PAST (IN)DISCRETIONS

~

CANADIAN FEDERAL AND PROVINCIAL FISCAL POLICY

BY RONALD KNEEBONE AND KENNETH MCKENZIE

Department of Economics, University of Calgary
2500 University Drive N.W. Calgary, Alberta T2N 1N4

Canadian Cataloguing in Publication Data

Kneebone, Ronald D. (Ronald David), 1955-
  Past (in)Discretions: Canadian Federal and Provincial Fiscal Policy

(Monograph series on public policy and public administration)
Includes bibliographical references.
ISBN 0-7727-8611-9
1. Fiscal policy – Canada. 2. Government spending policy – Canada.
3. Federal-provincial fiscal relations – Canada.   4. Canada – Economic policy –
  1945 I. McKenzie, Kenneth J. (Kenneth James), 1959-   .
II. University of Toronto. Centre for Public Management. III. Title. III. Series

HJ793.K55 1999   336.3'0971'09045   C99-932098-X

Printed for the University of Toronto Centre for Public Management by
University of Toronto Press.

PREFACE

In Past (In)Discretions: Canadian Federal and Provincial Fiscal Policy, Ronald Kneebone and Kenneth McKenzie tackle an extremely timely question. Because the country's eleven jurisdictions – one federal and ten provincial – all face the same monetary and exchange-rate constraints, but differ in the fiscal approaches they have taken to their debts and deficits, Canada offers a unique laboratory for comparing how various tax and expenditure regimes cure – and exacerbate – budgetary problems. Among the questions Kneebone and McKenzie tackle: Based on the Canadian experience, which approach works best? Cutting expenditures? Raising taxes? Or some combination thereof? Which approach is most sustainable? And which governments have the best track record?

Using a technique for isolating the discretionary component of government fiscal policy – focusing, in other words, on policy impulses that can be attributed to a government's own internal decision-making, not the impact of external economic factors – they examine federal and provincial fiscal records between 1962 and 1996. Over that time, they find, whenever Canadian governments introduced discretionary budget changes that increased a particular jurisdiction's deficit by over 1.5% of GDP – what Kneebone and McKenzie describe as a "very loose" fiscal stance – they almost always did so by raising expenditures, not by cutting taxes. By contrast, when introducing discretionary changes that reduced the deficit by the same amount (a "very tight" fiscal stance), governments tended historically to rely on a balanced mixture of tax increases and expenditure cuts, although more recently the latter have dominated in tight fiscal impulses. What this means is that, over time, a systemic tendency has emerged for governments to increase their size relative to the rest of the economy. In other words, discretionary fiscal policy leads to budgetary indiscretions.

In comparing federal and provincial strategies for combatting debt and deficit, the authors find that over the 1993-1996 period, federal expenditure cuts as a percentage of GDP amounted to much less than the average of all eleven governments. When it came to tax hikes, conversely, they write that "[f]or the federal government...deficit reduction efforts dominated by tax increases have historically tended to be futile, as these tax increases have tended to attract higher spending down the road." Only cutting federal program spending, they conclude, "will prove more likely to be associated with a lasting reduction in the federal deficit."

What about Saskatchewan, one might ask, where – at least in popular perception – the government has successfully attacked the deficit using tax increases instead of expenditure reduction? What the authors find is that, in fact, Saskatchewan actually drove its very tight fiscal stances in 1993 and 1994 with expenditure cuts. Indeed, during the 1993-96 period the government of Saskatchewan led all Canadian governments in expenditure-led deficit reduction. By contrast, the deficit reductions introduced by the Ontario government of Mike Harris did not prove so large as to be classified as very tight. And while the first two years of Ralph Klein's budget cuts in Alberta were "very tight," only in the first year, 1993, did expenditure cuts dominate. "The perception that the improvement in Alberta's finances is solely due to expenditure cuts," the authors write, "needs further examination."

Kneebone and McKenzie also document a very strong electoral-economic cycle in Canada. Although left-wing governments generally engage in looser fiscal policy than right-wing governments, even right-wing governments implemented discretionary increases in their primary deficits averaging 0.28 percentage points of GDP in election years. More generally, deficits go up during election years due to expenditure increases far more often than because of tax cuts.

Kneebone and McKenzie also offer a way of gauging the sustainability of fiscal polices over time. Here, they find that while the federal government has turned the corner – meaning that in 1996 it collected about $11 billion more in taxes than it needed to finance program spending and maintain the net debt/GDP ratio given current interest rates – the provinces, on average, have not. The reason: Unsustainable fiscal policies in the large provinces of B.C., Quebec and Ontario, where the actual tax rate in 1996 remained too low to finance existing levels of program spending without increasing the debt/GDP ratio.

Offering the first in-depth comparative analysis of the diverse strategies Canadian jurisdictions have used to combat their debt-and-deficit problems, Past (In)Discretions contains numerous insights into the historical record of various governments, cutting-edge analyses of breaking issues, and cautionary tales for the future that will prove invaluable to policymakers, analysts and commentators as they wrestle with Canada's fiscal policies in the years ahead. Past (In)Discretions is the ninth in a series of monographs in public policy published by the University of Toronto Centre for Public Management, and funded by a generous grant from the Donner Canadian Foundation.

Andrew Stark
Editor
Monograph Series on Public Policy
University of Toronto Centre for Public Management

ACKNOWLEDGEMENTS

Subject to the usual disclaimer, we would like to thank Herb Emery, John Forster, Dan Gordon, Robert Mansell, Tracy Snodden, Andrew Stark, two anonymous referees, and seminar participants at the Universities of Calgary and Alberta and for helpful comments. We, of course, are solely responsible for the opinions and interpretations offered in this monograph.

TABLE OF CONTENTS

CHAPTER ONE

INTRODUCTION

Over the past several years, Canadian governments at both the federal and provincial level have introduced policies intended to reduce the size of their budget deficits. A number of approaches have been tried. The government of Alberta is perceived as having adopted an approach characterized by a rapid reduction in expenditures with no tax increases. The government of Saskatchewan, on the other hand, is generally perceived as having eliminated a large deficit mainly via tax increases. The government of Ontario is cutting both spending and taxes and in so doing is taking a more gradual approach to deficit reduction than either of these provinces. The federal government has shown a preference for a "balanced approach" to deficit and debt reduction, relying on both tax increases and expenditure cuts. These different approaches to deficit reduction raise the question of whether one approach might be preferred to, or prove to be more successful than, the others. An investigation of this question, and the more general question of the nature of the fiscal policy choices that have been made in Canada recently and in the past, is one of the two broad goals of this study.

Our other goal is to examine the "sustainability" of government budget policies. That is, we address the question of whether or not the fiscal policy choices made by Canadian governments, recently and in the past, have represented feasible long-run choices; feasible in the sense that they could be left unaltered without causing debt to accumulate over the long-term. Our examination will therefore differ from the common approach of comparing fiscal stances of governments by presenting comparative figures on revenues, program expenditures, net debt, and the like. While such comparisons are useful, they are lacking in an important respect – they say nothing about whether or not a province's fiscal stance is *sustainable*, and therefore provide little insight into what changes in fiscal policy may be on the horizon.

Canada's public sector provides a unique "laboratory" in which to examine budget policies. All eleven governments – the ten provinces and the federal government – make budget choices essentially unfettered by constitutional rules that limit their involvement in the economy or their ability to run deficits and accumulate debt. This makes Canadian provinces very different from US states, for example, almost all of which operate under some form of constitutional restriction on the size of their budgets, their budget deficit and/or their accumulated debt.[1] Indeed, we will argue that Canadian provinces have taxing powers, spending responsibilities, and a freedom to run deficits and accumulate debt that is on par with OECD countries. A very important characteristic of this budget policy laboratory is the fact that all eleven governments share a common electoral system, all form budget policies within a reasonably common set of institutions using similar methods and approaches, and all experience common monetary and exchange rate shocks. Such commonality is important because differences in social and political institutions are thought by some to have an important influence on budget outcomes. It is often argued, for example, that electoral systems with proportional representation are inherently more unstable than pluralist electoral systems and hence are more likely to yield large deficits and high levels of government debt.[2] The degree of homogeneity of preferences across voters can also play a role in determining fiscal outcomes. Some authors, for example, argue that homogeneous voter preferences minimize social conflict and enable government to react more quickly and decisively to events having a negative impact upon the government budget deficit.[3] Thus the fact that voter preferences are likely to be more homogeneous across Canadian provinces than across countries is an important advantage researchers examining Canadian government budgets have over those using cross-country comparisons. What's more, it is well-known that budgetary choices are affected in an important way by monetary policy choices and exchange rate policies. Thus, the fact that all eleven Canadian governments operate within the constraint of a common set of monetary and exchange rate choices is an important advantage that allows us to clearly and easily isolate these influences from the effects of budget choices.

Our study of government budget policies in Canada will take advantage of this unique laboratory by examining the strategies of individual governments over time as well as by comparing those of the eleven governments at various points in time. Each of these dimensions is important. An examination of budget policies over time is important because, while it is tempting to think that deficit reduction efforts of the provinces and the federal government are a recent phenomenon, in point of fact they are not. Prior to 1975, when governments in Canada first began to run large and persistent deficits, provincial and federal government budget imbalances were consistently small and were as often positive as negative. Deficits and growing debt were not the norm. Indeed, the federal government rapidly reduced its debt/GDP ratio from a high of 111% in 1946 to a post-war low of under 16% in 1975. Thus, efforts at debt reduction are nothing new. The provinces also have had a long history of deficit reduction efforts; indeed, we will show that many provinces have been suffering the effects of high debts for decades. The second dimension of our study, that which compares budget policies across Canada's eleven fiscal authorities, is valuable because it provides us with the ability to compare how eleven governments responded to common events; events such as the increase in interest rates in the 1980s. Did they respond in a similar way to such events or did some respond differently from others? What was the result of these different responses?

The volume is divided into six chapters. Following this introductory chapter, Chapter 2 provides some background relevant to our study of government deficits and debt in Canada. We begin with a very brief overview of the structure of government fiscal policy in a Canadian context. The economic roles and responsibilities of the two levels of government, as well as the close connections between the levels of government due to the presence of intergovernmental grants, are summarized in this section. This is followed by an introduction to what is commonly referred to as the "simple arithmetic" of government deficits and debt. Here we identify the key determinants of the growth of deficits and debt and hence the determinants of the sustainability of budgetary choices. We then move on to a discussion of the costs and benefits of government debt. This section addresses the question of why we should be concerned about high levels of government debt and hence why we should be interested in finding effective ways of reducing debt. With this background, we conclude Chapter 2 with a brief summary of deficits and debt in Canada over the past four decades and highlight some of the key issues and events that have impacted upon the growth of government debt.

Chapter 3 looks at the issue of the sustainability of government fiscal policy. After introducing a methodology for measuring sustainability, we apply that methodology to the budgets of Canada's eleven fiscal authorities. Our methodology is based on the idea of a *sustainable tax rate*, which is the average tax rate (revenues as a percentage of GDP) required to maintain the current spending program (program spending as a percentage of GDP) and maintain the current net debt/GDP ratio.[4] Measuring the difference between the sustainable tax rate and the actual tax rate - called the *tax gap* - for each province and the federal government allows us to determine when budgets became unsustainable and the extent to which current budget stances remain so. Alternative choices for re-establishing sustainable budgets are investigated and their implications for tax rates and spending programs are drawn. We show that there have been some important, and perhaps surprising, differences in the evolution of the tax gap across the provinces over time, and that these differences coincide with episodes of falling or rising debt relative to the size of the economy. We also show that with a couple of important exceptions, individual provinces, and the federal government, began moving towards "more sustainable" budgetary policies in the mid-1990s, although there are some interesting and revealing differences in timing and magnitude. We also highlight the important role played by federal transfers in the sustainability of fiscal policy in some provinces.

In Chapter 4, we examine in considerable detail the characteristics of the fiscal policy choices that have been made by provincial and federal governments over the period 1961 to 1996. We begin by confronting an important analytical issue: to examine government budget policy choices we must first *identify* them. This is more difficult than it might seem because changes in economic conditions impact upon government budgets via income-sensitive revenues and expenditures (what are commonly referred to as "automatic stabilizers"). Thus, although Alberta, for example, quickly eliminated its deficit over the period from 1993 to 1996, and indeed has reported substantial budget surpluses for the past few years, the provincial budget has enjoyed the benefits of a strong economy. The federal budget has similarly benefited from strong economic growth and a rapid fall in debt servicing costs due to the fall in Canadian interest rates. How much, then, have deficits been reduced by automatic stabilizers, and how much by discretionary policy choices? Using a simple empirical approach, we separate changes in federal and provincial government budget positions due to changes in the business cycle (cyclical changes) from those due to policy choices (discretionary changes).[5]

Having identified budgetary policy changes in this way, we then investigate the *composition* of these various types of fiscal stances. Governments can reduce their budget deficits in three ways: by cutting spending, by raising taxes, or by some combination of spending cuts and tax increases. In which of these ways have Canadian governments reduced their deficits? Have they done so by cutting program spending and thus reducing government's role in the economy? Or have they done so by increasing taxes, thereby increasing government's role in the economy? A related question involves whether or not the commonly held perceptions regarding how the various governments have dealt with their deficit problems mentioned at the beginning of the chapter are true.

If the composition of budget changes has differed over time and across jurisdictions, this raises the question of whether certain approaches have proven more successful than others. This issue, too, is given close examination in Chapter 4. We are particularly interested in the question of whether some approaches to fiscal retrenchment are likely to have more or less "staying power" than other approaches.

Much of Chapter 4 also looks at broad regularities across all eleven governments. We also undertake more specific case studies of the budgetary policies of the federal government and the governments of Ontario and Alberta.

In Chapter 5, we examine various political influences on government fiscal policy, including the role of impending elections and the political ideology of the party in power. We find evidence of a marked electoral cycle in fiscal policy in Canada, especially in expenditures. Changes in discretionary government spending are significantly higher in election years than in non-election years. We also present evidence suggestive of strong partisan influences in Canadian fiscal policy. Left-wing governments introduce significantly higher amounts of discretionary spending than do right-wing governments.

The final chapter in the volume, Chapter 6, summarizes our findings and discusses some of the policy implications of our analysis.

We conclude this introductory chapter with a brief comment on the data we use to undertake much of our empirical analysis. There were basically two choices available to us, both of which have advantages and disadvantages. One approach would be to use public accounts data, which is based on federal and provincial budgets. The advantage of this data set is that it is both up to date, with budget figures up to 1997, and forward looking, with forecasts for 1998. The disadvantage is the accounting standards and definitions in the public accounts vary both over time and across provinces. For this reason we chose instead to rely on Financial Management System (FMS) data. This data set has the merit of using a consistent set of accounting standards and definitions both over time and across provinces and governments. This enables us to aggregate the provincial data where appropriate, and allows us to undertake confident comparisons between the provinces and levels of government. The disadvantage of using FMS data is that the most recent data is available only up to 1996. As such, some important fiscal initiatives that have taken place over the past two years, at both the federal and provincial level, are not reflected in our empirical analysis. While this is unfortunate, in our view, ultimately the analysis and conclusions that come out of it are only as good as the underlying data; it is thus very important to use a consistent data set that is comparable across governments and over time. Moreover, even though the FMS data set ends in 1996, we are still able to capture the 'turning of the corner' in Canadian fiscal policy that began in the early to mid-1990s.

PAST (IN)DISCRETIONS

CHAPTER TWO

BACKGROUND

We begin in this chapter by presenting background information that will provide a useful contextual framework for the rest of the volume. We start out with a brief overview of the general structure of government in Canada, including the major revenues and expenditures of both the federal and provincial governments. We then move on to a discussion of what is often referred to as the "simple arithmetic" of governments deficits and debt. This will serve as a useful analytical backdrop for Chapters 3 and 4. A third section briefly discusses the costs and benefits of government debt. We conclude with a brief historical overview of deficits, debt, and fiscal policy and Canada from 1961 to 1998.

2.1 The Structure of Government in Canada

In this section we provide a very brief discussion of the structure of government in Canada. Although the primary purpose of this volume is to study the broader issues of government deficits and debt, some knowledge of where the government gets its money, and what it does with it, will help place some of the discussion in the proper context.

Of course in Canada we have to be precise about what we are talking about when we talk about "the government." Canada has a *federal governmental structure*, which is to say that government activities take place at several levels: national (or federal), provincial, and local. The British North America (BNA) Act of 1867, Canada's constitution, sets out the taxing and spending responsibilities of the federal and provincial governments. The BNA Act has been amended several times, most recently in 1982; however the federalist structure of government in Canada has remained intact, and indeed is one of the defining features of the country. As we shall see, the federal structure of the country has important implications for the analysis of fiscal policy in Canada.

The federal government is responsible for matters of national interest, including things such as national defense and foreign policy, international trade, competition policy, criminal law, and money and banking. The federal government is also responsible for the delivery of some of Canada's social programs, including Employment Insurance (EI) and the Canada Pension Plan (CPP). For all intents and purposes, the federal government has unlimited taxing powers, as it is able to employ any system or mode of taxation it deems necessary.

The provinces are responsible for programs in the areas of health care, education, and welfare. They also have responsibility for natural resources within their boundaries and for civil law. Provinces have extensive taxing powers, although they are somewhat more limited than the federal government. Compared to most other federations, including the United States, Canadian provinces have a great deal of power and fiscal autonomy. Indeed, the provinces account for about half of the activities undertaken by the public sector in Canada, and so, in aggregate, are as important as the federal government. Local governments - cities, towns and municipalities - are creatures of the provinces, and receive all of their spending and taxing authority from the provinces.

An important aspect of the federal form of government in Canada is the role of *transfers* from the federal government to the provinces. Although the federal government is not directly responsible for programs related to health, education and welfare, its has been able to exercise substantial influence over the provinces in these areas through "the power of the purse." The most important transfer program is the *Canada Health and Social Transfer* (CHST). Although the CHST is ostensibly to be used to finance provincial programs related to health, welfare and post-secondary education, it is in fact a block grant that simply enters general provincial revenues and may be used as the provincial governments see fit. The CHST was introduced in 1996 to replace transfers under the *Established Program Financing* (EPF) program for hospitals and post-secondary education, and the *Canada Assistance Plan* (CAP) for welfare. Both EPF and CAP were conditional grants that had to be spent in their respective areas.

Another important feature of the Canadian federation is the role of *equalization payments*. Under this program, the federal government provides general purpose transfers to the so-called "have-not" provinces so that they may provide government services of a quality roughly comparable to the "have" provinces. The "have" provinces – those that do not receive equalization payments – are British Columbia, Alberta and Ontario. The remaining provinces all receive various amounts of equalization payments, depending upon their need. The Yukon and North West Territories receive similar payments under a separate program.

2.1.1 The Federal Government

The federal government collects about half of the taxes in the economy. It raises this money in a number of ways, and finds even more ways to spend it.

Table 2-1 shows the total revenues of the federal government in 1996. Total revenues in this year were $135 billion. This is a big number. To bring it down to earth we can divide it by the Canadian population, which was about 30 million in 1996. We then find that the average Canadian paid about $4,517 to the federal government in 1996; or about $18,068 for a typical family of four.

The largest source of revenue for the federal government is the personal income tax, which accounts for almost half of total federal revenues. In 1996, almost 14 million Canadian taxpayers filled out a tax form to determine how much income tax they owed the government. Personal income taxes account for almost half of total federal revenue, about $2,110 per capita or just over $4,500 per taxpayer.

The next most important revenue source for the federal government is the payroll tax used to finance the Employment Insurance (EI) program. A *payroll tax* is a tax on the wages that a firm pays its workers. In Canada, EI payroll taxes are split between employers and employees. Table 2-1 shows that the average Canadian paid about $653 in EI payroll taxes in 1996. Another program that is financed by payroll taxes is the *Canada Pension Plan* (CPP) which provides pensions to all retired Canadians. CPP payroll taxes, which amounted to about $15 billion in 1996, are not included in Table 2-1 because it operates under a separate budget.

Table 2-1	Revenues of the Federal Government: 1996		
Tax	**Amount (Billions)**	**Amount per Person**	**Percent of Revenues**
Personal Income Taxes	$63.5	$2110	47%
Employment Insurance Payroll Taxes	19.6	657	14
Corporate Income Taxes	15.8	527	12
Goods and Services Tax	16.9	593	12
Excise Taxes & Duties	10.1	347	8
Other	**9.5**	**317**	**7**
Total	**$135.5**	**$4517**	**100%**

Source: Federal Budget Papers, 1997.

Next in magnitude is the corporate income tax, which accounts for 12 percent of federal tax revenues. The Goods and Services Tax (GST) also accounts for about 12 percent of federal government revenues. Each Canadian paid almost $600 in GST in 1996. Excise and custom duties cost an additional $357 per person, accounting for 8 percent of federal revenues. Excise taxes are sales taxes imposed on specific commodities, such as gasoline, cigarettes, and alcohol. Custom duties are taxes applied to goods imported into the country. Total taxes on the sale of goods and services (the GST plus excise and custom duties) account for 20 percent of federal revenues, or almost $1000 per person.

Table 2-2 shows the spending of the federal government in 1996. Total spending was almost $155 billion, or $5,150 per person. About 30 percent of this was interest paid on the federal government's debt. The remaining 70 percent was devoted to *program spending* – the sum of all expenditure other than debt services costs – which amounts to $3,633 per person.

Aside from debt payments, the single largest expenditure category is payments to the elderly, which account for 14 percent of total federal government expenditures. These include payments under the *Old Age Security* (OAS) and *Guaranteed Income Supplement* (GIS) programs, which are transfer programs designed to provide income support for the elderly. Payments under the CPP in 1996 were about $22 billion. Note that this

Table 2-2	Spending of the Federal Government: 1996		
	Amount (Billions)	Amount per Person	Percent of Spending
Elderly Benefits	$21.6	$72	14%
Employment Insurance	13.1	437	8
CHST	14.9	497	10
Equalization	8.5	283	5
Defence	9.6	320	6
Subsidies and Other Transfers	18.3	610	12
Other	23.0	767	15
Total Program Spending	109.0	3633	70
Debt Service	**45.5**	**1500**	**30**
Total Spending	**$154.5**	**$5150**	**100%**

Source: Federal Budget Papers, 1997.

is somewhat less than the $15 billion in CPP payroll taxes collected. This shortfall has been the subject of some concern and has precipitated changes in 1997 to the CPP in order to make the plan more sustainable.

The next largest category is subsidies and other transfers. These include payments under the *Infrastructure Program* to help shore up Canada's roads, bridges and sewer systems (as well as the odd hockey arena), subsidies to businesses, international aid, programs related to science and technology, and payments related to Indians and Inuit.

Transfers to the provinces under the CHST account for 10 percent of federal program expenditures; equalization payments account for an additional 5 percent. Total transfers to the provinces thus make up about 15 percent of federal government expenditures.

The Employment Insurance (EI) program cost $13.1 billion in 1996, accounting for 8 percent of federal expenditures. It is interesting to compare this figure to the payroll taxes collected by the federal government for EI, which amounted to $19.6 billion. This means that government receipts for EI exceeded government payments by $6.5 billion, a considerable surplus. The prevalence of a sizable EI surplus over the past several years has prompted many commentators to call for a reduction in EI payroll taxes.

National defense accounted for 6 percent of federal expenditures in 1996. It is interesting to compare this figure to the US, where roughly 18% of federal government expenditures are related to national defense.

You might have noticed that the total spending of the federal government shown in Table 2-2 exceeds total revenues shown in Table 2-1. This, of course, accounts for the federal budget deficit, which was about $19 billion in 1996. We will, of course, have a lot more to say about the federal deficit throughout the course of the volume.

2.1.2 Provincial Governments

Provincial governments in Canada also account for roughly 50 percent of taxes paid. Here we take a quick look at how they obtain tax revenue and how they spend it.

Table 2-3 shows the aggregate revenues of provincial governments in Canada. Total revenues in 1996 were about $167 billion, or $5,553 per person. Note, however, that $25 billion of this consists of transfers from the federal government; this is 15 percent of total provincial revenues. Provincial *own source revenues* therefore amounted to $142 billion, or $4,733 per person.

Like the federal government, the single most important source of revenues for the provinces are personal income taxes, which account for 27% of revenues, or $1,487 per person. With the exception of Quebec, all of the provinces 'piggy-back' on the federal personal income tax system via the Tax Collection Agreement (TCA), with provincial income taxes determined as a percentage of federal income taxes – the so-called "tax on tax" approach. Quebec's system mirrors the federal system closely. Changes to the TCA effective in 2001 give provinces the option of levying their taxes directly on the federal base – the so-called "tax on base" approach. Alberta has announced its intentions to move to this approach in 2002; Ontario and Manitoba have also expressed interest in this possibility.

Table 2-3	Revenues of Provincial Governments: 1996		
	Amount (Billions)	Amount per Person	Percent of Spending
Personal Income Tax	$44.6	$1487	27%
Sales Tax	21.7	723	13
Transfers	25.4	847	15
Health Levies	11.8	393	7
Excise Taxes	8.6	287	5
Corporate Income Tax	8.8	293	5
Natural Resource Revenues	7.5	250	4
Other	38.2	127	23
Total	$166.6	$5553	100%

Source: Statistics Canada, Provincial Government Revenues and Expenditures, CANSIM Matrix No. 2781.

Sales taxes are the next largest revenue source for the provinces, accounting for 13 percent of provincial revenues. All of the provinces except Alberta levy sales taxes collected at the retail level.

Provincial health levies make up 7 percent of provincial revenues. Most provinces levy a payroll tax, paid by employers, to help fund health programs. Saskatchewan levies no such tax, and Alberta and British Columbia impose lump sum health care premiums on a yearly basis, paid by employees.

Another source of revenue that can be important for some provinces is natural resource levies, arising from royalties imposed on the production of oil and gas, and taxes imposed on the income from mining or forestry. In aggregate, these revenues account for only 4 percent of provincial revenues, but this proportion is substantially higher in some provinces, such as Alberta which relies heavily on oil and gas royalties.

PAST (IN)DISCRETIONS

Table 2-4 shows the total spending of provincial governments in 1996 and its breakdown among the major categories.

Expenditures on health, social services and education – "The Big Three" – account for the lion's share of provincial spending – 63 percent of total spending in 1996, or $3,677 per person. Health is the biggest single component, followed by social services and education. Social services include expenditures on welfare programs for the poor. Education includes expenditures on primary, secondary, and post-secondary institutions.

Provincial government expenditures on the protection of persons and property, transportation and communication, and general services together account for 11 percent of provincial spending, while debt service charges account for 16 percent.

Notice that in aggregate provincial spending exceeded provincial revenues – the aggregate provincial deficit was $8.2 billion in 1996.

Table 2-4	Spending of Provincial Governments: 1996		
	Amount (Billions)	Amount per Person	Percent of Spending
Health	$45.3	$1510	26%
Social Services	33.6	1120	19
Education	31.4	1047	18
Protection	4.9	163	3
Transportation and Communication	6.7	223	4
General Services	7.5	250	4
Debt Service	27.9	930	16
Other	**17.5**	**583**	**10**
Total	**$174.8**	**$5800**	**100%**

Source: Statistics Canada, Provincial Government Revenues and Expenditures, CANSIM Matrix No. 2781.

2.2 The Simple Arithmetic of Government Deficits and Debt

To help us understand what causes government deficits and debt to grow, it is useful to introduce some simple and intuitive accounting relationships relevant to government budgets. A mathematical understanding of some very basic relationships goes a long way to illuminating the unavoidable "truth and consequences" of government debt. We will exploit these relationships further in Chapter 3 when we discuss the sustainability of fiscal policy.

A government *budget imbalance* is simply the difference between what the government collects in tax revenue and what it spends during a fiscal year. If that difference is positive – that is, the government collects more in tax revenue than it spends – the government is said to have realized a *budget surplus*. A *budget deficit* arises when the government spends more than it collects in tax revenue. The sum of all budget surpluses and deficits that have been incurred since it became a legal entity defines that government's *debt*.

Another important distinction regards the difference between *gross* and *net* debt. Gross debt is the total of all government financial liabilities. However, governments also accumulate financial assets either as an explicit policy measure, as, for example, in the case of the Alberta Heritage Saving Trust Fund, or to provide "working capital" for the every day business of government. These financial assets provide a rate of return which enters general government revenues. These financial assets can be quite sizeable relative to the size of financial liabilities, particularly at the provincial level. In this volume we are interested primarily in the net debt of the federal and provincial governments, which is the difference between financial assets and liabilities.

As is the case with households, the economic consequences of government debt depends on its size relative to its ability to pay interest on that debt, as represented by the total income generated in the economy. For this reason, government deficits and debt are usually expressed as a fraction of gross domestic product (GDP). Gross domestic product measures the dollar value of all sources of income and all expenditures in the economy. Since taxes are mainly applied against either income or expenditures, GDP is a rough measure of the tax base. Thus, a government debt of 50 billion dollars might sound large until it is measured relative to GDP, the collective income of all those in the economy ultimately responsible for that debt. If GDP is $500 billion, a debt of $50 billion, equal to 10% of GDP, seems small. At an interest rate of 8%, only $4 billion, or 0.8% of the economy's annual income, must be spent to pay interest on that debt. If, however, GDP is itself only $50 billion, that same debt, now equal to 100% of GDP, seems onerous indeed. At the same 8% interest rate, 8% of the economy's annual income must be spent to pay interest on the debt.

As is the case for households, governments face a budget constraint requiring that expenditures equal all sources of revenue. Governments generate revenue via taxation and by selling bonds. Thus, a deficit, the result of spending being greater than tax revenue, is paid for by the sale of government bonds. Similarly, a surplus, the result of tax revenue being greater than spending, results in the retirement of outstanding debt. The government's budget constraint over the coming year can be written simply as:

$$d = g - t + rb \qquad (2.1)$$

where d=deficit as a fraction of GDP, g=program spending as a fraction of GDP, t=tax revenue as a fraction of GDP, r=the interest rate on outstanding government debt, b=B/GDP=net government debt at the beginning of the year as a percentage of GDP. The last term in equation (2.1) measures the cost of paying interest on existing debt (net of interest earned on financial assets). The amount g-t is referred to as the government's *primary deficit*; the difference between program (non-interest) spending and tax revenue (all as a fraction of GDP). The primary deficit does not incorporate the debt service component of government spending, and hence identifies this year's addition to outstanding debt. Equation (2.1), then, simply states that the deficit in the coming year is equal to the cost of servicing outstanding debt plus the net addition to debt in that year. It should be noted that as written, equation (2.1) is forward looking in the sense that it describes the deficit that will occur over the coming year. This is an issue to which we return in Chapter 3.

Using equation (2.1), the percentage change in a government's net debt/GDP ratio can be expressed in the following way;

$$\Delta b = g - t + (r - y)b \qquad (2.2)$$

where the symbol Δ means 'change in.' Thus Δb is the change in the net debt/GDP ratio over the coming year. The symbol y defines the rate of growth in GDP. The first two terms on the right hand side of equation (2.2) indicate that a primary deficit $(g - t)$ adds to accumulated debt. The last term indicates that even if the primary deficit $(g - t)$ is zero, the ratio of debt to GDP can change. This is so because paying interest on outstanding debt increases the numerator of the debt/GDP ratio and because economic growth increases the size of the denominator. Whether the ratio of debt to GDP rises or falls depends on whether the interest rate exceeds the rate of growth in GDP.

These simple equations make clear that there are three key sources of growth for a government's net debt/GDP ratio. One is the primary deficit. A positive value for the primary deficit indicates that program spending exceeds tax revenue (both as a fraction of GDP) so that over the course of the fiscal year the government will make a net addition to its debt. A negative value for the primary deficit indicates the opposite; tax revenue will exceed program spending so that in this fiscal year the government will make a net reduction to its debt. The second key variable is the interest rate payable on outstanding debt. As this interest rate increases, the annual cost of servicing a given debt increases. If nothing else changes, the annual deficit grows and debt accumulates more quickly. The third key variable is the rate of growth in GDP. The more quickly GDP grows, the smaller will be the debt to GDP ratio. As equation (2.2) indicates, it is the relative magnitudes of the interest rate payable on government debt (r) and the rate of growth in GDP (y) which is key. Intuitively, if the interest rate exceeds the rate of growth, the addition to debt resulting from servicing outstanding debt exceeds the increase in GDP due to economic growth. Thus, the ratio of debt to GDP rises. In Chapter 3, we will modify and exploit the simple arithmetic of government debt to discuss the sustainability of fiscal policy at both the federal and provincial level in Canada.

2.3 The Costs and Benefits of Government Debt

Why should we be concerned about government debt? This is obviously an important question for us to address, since this volume is concerned with the issue of debt reduction. If government debt has little consequence for economic well-being, or indeed, if it offers net economic benefits, then why should we be concerned about investigating ways of reducing it?

It is generally acknowledged that the ability of government to maintain a level of debt affords society both benefits and costs. The purpose of this section is to briefly review the major costs and benefits of government debt. By doing so, we hope to provide some background for understanding why most analysts judge the current levels of government debt in Canada to be of concern.

Although it is recognized that there are a number of important benefits to be enjoyed by societies that allow their governments to experience *periodic* budget surpluses and deficits, there is only one generally recognized benefit from allowing governments to maintain a *permanent* level of debt; it allows a sharing of the costs and benefits of government expenditures across generations.[1]

The argument for this runs as follows: Economies operate efficiently when those who receive the benefit from some expenditure also pay the cost of that expenditure. Applying this doctrine becomes difficult in cases when the benefits of expenditures reach across generations. Many government expenditures face this problem. That is, many government expenditures are on goods and services that benefit not only the current generation of taxpayers but will also benefit future generations. Examples of such expenditures include government spending on airports, roads, sewers and national parks. Another example is the cost of financing a war or a peace-keeping mission. In cases like these, economic efficiency requires that future generations somehow be made to share the cost of a current expenditure. Unless this is done, the current taxpaying generation will tend to vote for an under-supply of the expenditure in question. An effective way of enabling future generations to share in the cost of financing a current expenditure is for government to run a deficit. The size of the deficit should be such that the cost to each generation of servicing the debt is equal to the amount of benefit such expenditures provide to that generation.

Against this benefit, society must weigh the cost of allowing government to maintain a permanent level of debt. The most important cost is that a permanent level of government debt reduces the capital stock and hence slows the rate of economic growth. It does this in two related ways: by reducing the supply of savings available to the private sector and by increasing the cost of borrowing to the private sector. These effects are due to the fact that financial markets convert household savings into investment and capital goods. The financing of government deficits involves the sale of government bonds to households, and households make these purchases with their savings. In this way, household savings are diverted toward the financing of government expenditures rather than toward the purchase of capital goods. What is more, in order to sell their bonds, government must make them attractive to potential purchasers. They do so by selling bonds with interest rates that are competitive with those offered by the private sector. The more bonds that governments seek to sell, the higher must be the interest rate offered in order to attract purchasers. In this way, higher government debt leads to higher interest rates and consequently less investment in capital. Via both these channels, a higher level of government debt leads to less private sector capital formation and hence to slower private sector economic growth.[2]

How might we estimate the cost borne by Canadians as a result of government debt lowering the capital stock? A "back of the envelope" calculation suggests that this cost amounts to about 2.5% of net national income.[3] That is, the existence of this debt costs Canadians a permanent 2.5% decrease in their living standards. In 1998, this amounted to a permanent loss of about $16 billion or roughly $500 per year for every man, woman and child in Canada.

Another important cost of a permanent level of government debt is the interest paid on that debt. If we ignore those interest payments that flow to foreigners, expenditures on debt servicing costs simply represent a transfer from taxpayers to debt holders. There would be no net cost to Canadians if this transfer was accomplished via lump sum (non-distortionary) taxes. In fact, of course, the taxes used to achieve this transfer are distortionary and thus impose additional costs on society. Economists refer to the additional cost arising from the use of distortionary taxes as the "deadweight loss" of taxation. These deadweight losses arise because taxes change relative costs and prices in the economy, causing people to change their behaviour. A recent estimate of the deadweight loss per dollar of tax revenue collected in Canada is that it is in the vicinity of sixty cents.[4] If we assume a real interest rate on government debt of 4%, then the deadweight loss per dollar of debt is ($0.6 x 0.04) 2.4 cents. In 1998, the combined debts of the federal and provincial governments amounted to about $850 billion. Thus the deadweight loss due to the costs of servicing that debt amounted to about $20 billion or roughly $700 per man, woman and child in Canada per year.

Admittedly, our estimates of the cost borne by Canadians as a result of the federal and provincial governments carrying a total of about $850 billion of net debt are only rough guesses. Nonetheless, the amounts are large enough – a total of $36 billion or $1200 per person per year – that it is difficult to believe that refinements of our calculations would alter the conclusion that the costs borne by Canadians are very large indeed.[5] What is more, we have not included in this calculation other costs that are more difficult to quantify. One such cost is that a large debt, especially when owed to foreigners, makes a country vulnerable to crises of international confidence. Canada recently felt the sting of such a loss of confidence in the form of higher interest rates when, in 1995, credit rating agencies down-graded Canada's foreign currency denominated debt. Another important cost is the loss of fiscal flexibility. The high debt of the federal government has limited its ability to fund new policy initiatives and, indeed, may have prevented it from continuing to fund established social programs. As we shall see later in the volume (in Chapter 4), one way in which the federal government has responded to high debt service payments is by cutting transfers to the provinces. In a very real way, then, the high debt of the federal government has had serious consequences for intergovernmental relations and the structure of Canadian federalism.

The fact that government debt generates both benefits and costs to society suggests that the optimal amount of government debt is not zero. In fact, the very existence of costs and benefits implies an optimal amount of government debt. Beyond the general agreement amongst economists that an amount of debt equal to 100% of GDP is too much, and zero debt is too little, there is little agreement as to the optimal level of debt.[6]

A different perspective on the question of the optimal level of debt considers the role of politics.[7] If the objective of democratically elected policy-makers is to set a budget in a way that maximizes political support, and if support for the government increases with increases in program spending and declines for increases in taxes, then the politically optimal budget will make use of all types of revenue, including borrowing. In particular, governments seeking to maximize their political support will utilize revenue up to the point where the marginal political opposition per dollar of tax revenue raised is equalized. So long as deficit financing does not face extraordinarily high political costs, it will be part of a politically optimal budget. Deficit reduction will be favoured by politicians only when the political price of raising revenue via deficit finance becomes greater than that from taxation or from expenditure cuts. Since at some point a growing debt/GDP ratio must become large enough that the costs of servicing that debt either crowd out other types of government expenditure or demand an unbearable level of taxation, eventually the political price of further deficits becomes prohibitive. At this point, the political benefits of deficit reduction overwhelm the benefits of deficit increases and politicians will propose programs of deficit reduction. In some sense, then, there may be a maximum level of debt beyond which political expediency will demand adoption of a more fiscally prudent course and debt reduction.

Considerations such as these suggest, then, that the "optimal" level of government debt has at least two dimensions – the amount that is optimal for balancing the *economic* benefits and costs of debt, and the amount that is optimal for balancing *political* costs and benefits. While it is very difficult to quantify these two dimensions, in Chapter 5 we do show how political considerations such as looming elections and the party affiliation of the government have played a role in determining the fiscal policy choices of governments in Canada.

2.4 Deficits and Debt, 1962-98

This section briefly summarizes the budgetary experiences of the federal and ten provincial governments over the period 1962 to 1998. Our primary purpose here is to describe the impact of the three key determinants of budget deficits that we discussed in section 2.2.

As we noted in section 2.2, all else equal, government debt/GDP ratios grow larger over time if the interest rate paid on outstanding debt exceeds the rate of growth in GDP, and they grow smaller over time if the opposite is true. Figure 2-1 presents information on the growth rate of GDP and the interest rate paid on outstanding government debt over the period 1962-98.

These data are directly relevant to the federal government in that the GDP growth rate is the growth rate of the entire country's GDP and the

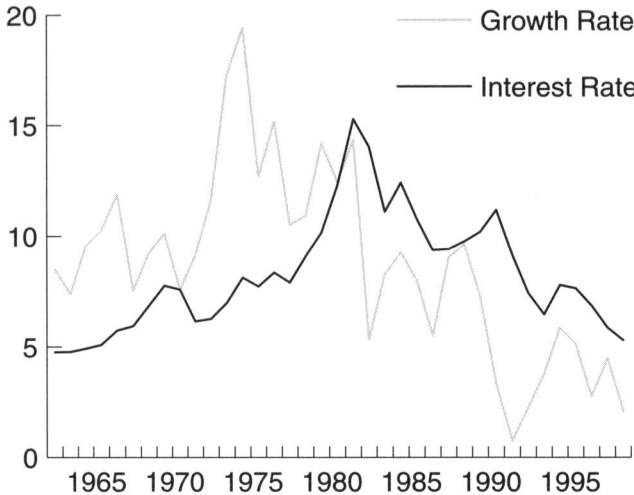

Figure 2-1: The Growth Rate versus the Interest Rate, 1962-98

Data on the GDP growth rate is based on seasonally adjusted quarterly data expressed at annual rates (CANSIM series D16439). The 1998 observation for the GDP growth rate is based on the first three quarters of that year. The value of the relevant nominal interest rate was determined by matching the average term to maturity of federal debt (CANSIM series B2430) to the interest rate paid on Government of Canada bonds of that maturity. Over our sample period, the average term to maturity ranged from a low of 45.6 months (in 1975) to a high of 98.3 months (in 1963). Thus we used either the bond yield on 3-5 year Government of Canada bonds (B14010) or the bond yield on 5-10 year bonds (B14011). Data for 1998 is based on the first eleven months of that year.

interest rate is that paid on outstanding federal government debt. The relevant interest rate for a province will tend to be higher than that paid on federal debt mainly because provinces have less diversified tax bases than the national government. The less diversified the tax base, and the higher the outstanding debt of a province, the higher the interest rate it must pay on its debt. Governments of economically large provinces with more diversified tax bases, like Ontario, and provinces with low levels of net debt, like Alberta, pay a rate of interest only slightly higher (typically about 0.5 percentage points) than that paid by the federal government. The government of Newfoundland, on the other hand, pays an interest rate on its debt that may be two percentage points higher than that paid by the federal government. Growth rates of GDP will also differ across provinces. Despite these differences, the data plotted in Figure 2-1 are broadly relevant to all governments in Canada.

Figure 2-1 shows that the beginning of the 1980s marked an important event in the evolution of government debt in Canada. Whereas during the 1960s and 1970s the rate of GDP growth exceeded the average interest rate paid on outstanding government debt, the opposite became true at the beginning of the 1980s. To the extent that these values are exogenous to fiscal policy choices, these data show that events largely outside the control of Canada's eleven fiscal authorities conspired, in and around 1980, to make it much more difficult to control the growth in their debt/GDP ratios than had previously been the case.[8] The relationship between interest rates and growth rates would thereafter cause debt/GDP ratios to grow over time. To prevent this growth, it would be necessary for governments to take fiscal actions to reduce their primary deficits (or increase their primary surpluses). We will return to this issue later on in Chapter 3.

Table 2-5 contains data on government deficits, primary deficits, and debt servicing costs, all as a fraction of provincial GDP for four sub-periods. Table 2-6 presents data on provincial and federal government net debt/GDP ratios. The variation in debt/GDP ratios reflects the relative influences on the debt/GDP ratio of interest rates, GDP growth rates, and changes in primary deficits. By referring to these two tables, along with Figure 2-1, we will be able to describe the impact on the federal budget and those of the provinces of three key determinants of budget deficits. We begin with a discussion of the federal government's finances.

Given the high profile of the federal government's recent efforts at deficit reduction, it might be surprising that the high deficits of the 1980s and early 1990s were, in fact, aberrations in federal fiscal behaviour. From Table 2-5, we see that during the 1960s, the federal government was the very model of fiscal prudence.[9] A primary surplus equal to just under 2% of GDP was sufficient to pay for the cost of servicing the government's outstanding debt. As a result, the average value of the deficit/GDP ratio was about zero during this decade. This, plus the favourable relative magnitudes of the interest rate and growth rate, illustrated in Figure 2-1, enabled the federal government to reduce its debt/GDP ratio from 31% in 1960/61 to 21.5% by 1969/70.

In the first half of the 1970s the federal government continued the pattern of the 1960s – modest deficits offset by modest surpluses and a steady primary surplus. These fiscal choices, along with a favourable combination of values for the interest rate and the growth rate, caused the debt/GDP ratio to fall to 16% by 1974/75.

The second half of the decade witnessed a dramatic change in the budgetary choices of the federal government. Small budget imbalances, both positive and negative, were replaced by an unbroken string of deficits averaging over 3% of GDP. Primary deficits replaced primary sur-

Table 2-5: Budget Measures, Decade Averages, 1961-96

	1961-69	1970-79	1980-89	1990-96
Newfoundland				
Deficit/GDP	4.35	3.15	2.02	0.42
Primary Deficit/GDP	2.68	-1.13	-3.99	-5.45
Debt Service/GDP	1.67	4.27	6.00	5.87
PEI				
Deficit/GDP	1.31	-0.55	-0.23	2.06
Primary Deficit/GDP	-0.82	-3.21	-4.10	-2.47
Debt Service/GDP	2.13	2.66	3.87	4.53
Nova Scotia				
Deficit/GDP	0.05	0.65	1.63	1.14
Primary Deficit/GDP	-1.45	-1.68	-2.24	-3.47
Debt Service/GDP	1.50	2.33	3.87	4.61
New Brunswick				
Deficit/GDP	0.66	0.62	1.42	0.62
Primary Deficit/GDP	-0.77	-1.28	-1.93	-4.24
Debt Service/GDP	1.43	1.90	3.35	4.87
Quebec				
Deficit/GDP	0.67	1.03	1.53	1.63
Primary Deficit/GDP	0.24	-0.06	-1.42	-2.04
Debt Service/GDP	0.43	1.09	2.95	3.67
Ontario				
Deficit/GDP	0.15	1.00	0.81	2.71
Primary Deficit/GDP	0.63	-0.22	-1.15	-0.21
Debt Service/GDP	0.48	1.22	1.97	2.50
Manitoba				
Deficit/GDP	0.09	0.43	2.39	0.95
Primary Deficit/GDP	-0.63	-1.04	-1.83	-4.74
Debt Service/GDP	0.72	1.48	4.23	5.69
Saskatchewan				
Deficit/GDP	-0.56	-1.23	1.63	0.37
Primary Deficit/GDP	-1.72	-2.55	-2.48	-5.47
Debt Service/GDP	1.16	1.33	4.11	5.83
Alberta				
Deficit/GDP	1.65	-2.74	-1.43	0.52
Primary Deficit/GDP	1.32	-3.52	-2.70	-2.00
Debt Service/GDP	0.33	0.78	1.27	2.52
B.C.				
Deficit/GDP	-1.05	-0.95	0.41	0.98
Primary Deficit/GDP	-1.14	-1.26	-0.82	-1.24
Debt Service/GDP	0.09	0.31	1.23	2.22
Federal Gov't.				
Deficit/GDP	0.00	1.44	4.52	3.55
Primary Deficit/GDP	-1.89	-0.82	-0.16	-2.15
Debt Service/GDP	0.43	1.09	2.95	3.67

Note: *Data is measured on a calendar year basis. A negative value indicates a budget surplus.*
Sources: *Provincial government revenue and expenditure data are from CANSIM matrices 6769-6778 and 9085-9094. Federal revenue and expenditure data are from matrices 6671 and 9070.*

Table 2-6: Net Debt to GDP Ratios, 1969/70 to 1995/96

	1970	1971	1972	1973	1974	1975	1976	1977	1978	1979	1980	1981	1982
Newfoundland	30.4	30.3	35.5	37.0	35.7	34.2	35.1	38.3	39.7	45.5	42.0	40.3	37.1
PEI	32.4	32.0	31.9	29.0	22.8	21.5	22.3	16.3	19.8	18.9	16.9	17.7	15.0
Nova Scotia	13.0	14.0	13.7	12.5	11.4	10.8	10.9	10.6	11.5	13.1	13.3	15.4	18.4
New Brunswick	20.4	21.1	20.4	19.1	16.2	15.9	17.8	18.1	20.9	20.0	16.6	20.2	19.2
Quebec	12.7	13.7	15.2	16.0	16.0	15.4	17.0	17.9	19.7	20.7	21.9	24.7	21.2
Ontario	5.5	5.1	7.2	7.1	7.3	8.1	9.5	9.9	11.2	12.1	11.5	11.5	11.5
Manitoba	1.0	-0.1	0.4	0.4	0.6	1.6	3.8	5.5	11.2	10.8	9.3	9.2	9.8
Saskatchewan	-2.7	-4.5	-4.6	-5.2	-6.3	-7.8	-8.4	-7.7	-7.9	-8.2	-7.9	-7.5	-7.0
Alberta	-5.5	-4.9	-2.6	-2.0	-3.5	-7.9	-9.8	-12.5	-18.3	-24.9	-25.1	-24.1	-24.4
British Columbia	-5.6	-8.5	-9.0	-8.8	-8.7	-7.4	-4.5	-4.5	-5.5	-5.6	-5.7	-5.4	-4.1
Federal Government	21.5	20.6	19.6	18.3	16.7	16.1	16.4	16.3	20.7	24.0	25.9	27.4	27.6

	1983	1984	1985	1986	1987	1988	1989	1990	1991	1992	1993	1994	1995
Newfoundland	37.4	39.3	40.3	42.4	43.0	41.7	38.1	38.2	39.9	42.0	46.6	50.0	51.0
PEI	16.8	14.6	14.4	14.8	14.4	14.8	15.0	14.5	15.8	17.5	18.3	23.3	29.3
Nova Scotia	20.2	21.0	22.8	24.3	24.5	24.0	23.1	28.0	28.5	30.8	37.8	43.2	47.0
New Brunswick	23.1	23.7	24.1	25.6	24.1	24.8	23.0	21.5	22.5	24.8	26.0	27.8	28.5
Quebec	25.0	21.0	22.6	25.5	25.6	24.4	22.3	21.5	21.9	24.1	27.1	29.7	32.9
Ontario	15.4	11.1	10.8	12.0	11.6	10.9	9.8	11.5	12.1	15.9	20.0	24.0	25.7
Manitoba	12.4	15.4	16.5	22.0	26.5	28.6	23.5	22.1	22.3	25.2	27.4	30.7	28.8
Saskatchewan	-4.7	-2.4	0.6	4.9	12.2	15.5	16.6	17.3	17.4	31.8	35.1	38.9	36.6
Alberta	-22.0	-22.3	-23.0	-21.5	-17.4	-14.7	-10.9	-7.2	-5.3	-2.3	3.9	5.3	3.7
British Columbia	-1.7	0.2	1.4	2.5	3.2	2.8	1.2	0.2	0.6	3.4	5.4	5.4	5.0
Federal Government	33.8	40.0	46.7	50.5	54.1	54.7	54.5	55.3	58.3	62.7	67.3	70.8	72.2

Notes: *Debt is measured on a fiscal year basis (year ending March 31st). Negative values indicate a net asset position. Provincial data is based on FMS conventions while federal data is based on SNA conventions. For the provinces, net debt is financial liabilities minus direct liabilities. Liabilities to employee pension plans are not included in direct liabilities. The net assets of the QPP plan are subtracted from Quebec's net debt. This allows for comparison with other provinces since CPP assets and liabilities do not appear in the net debts of the other provinces.*

pluses. Despite the fact that the relative sizes of the interest rate and growth rate still favoured reductions in the debt/GDP ratio, by decade's end the federal debt/GDP ratio had climbed to 24%.

Most of the growth in the federal debt/GDP ratio from its low in 1974/75 occurred since 1980. As we have already noted, the reversal of the relative values of the interest rate paid on federal debt and the rate of GDP growth would, all else equal, cause the debt/GDP ratio to grow larger. Behind this reversal was the Bank of Canada's decision to adopt the U.S. Federal Reserve System's policy of a tight monetary policy beginning in 1980. Not only did this policy drive interest rates upward, but it precipitated a recession that dramatically reduced the growth rate of nominal GDP. The effects of recession on the primary balance – recessions cause tax revenues to fall, expenditures on programs such as unemployment insurance to increase, and the primary deficit to grow – in conjunction with the unfavourable combination of a high interest rate and a low rate of economic growth, was a recipe for high deficits and a rapid growth in the debt/GDP ratio.

Events outside the control of the federal government therefore conspired to produce conditions ripe for a rapid increase in debt during the early 1980s. This leaves the question of whether the federal government took decisive action over budget choices under its control to halt, or slow down, the accumulation of debt. Providing the tools to answer this question is one goal of this volume. We will address this issue head on in Chapter 4 where we discuss the discretionary fiscal policy choices of the federal government. The data in Table 2-5 tell us only the effect of policy choices together with the effect of economic conditions on government budgets; the data do not separate these two sources of change. In Chapter 4 we will discuss a method for doing just that and present the results.

To preview our results and discussion in Chapter 4, we will show that during the early 1980s, the federal government introduced discretionary policy changes that substantially *worsened* its budgetary position. Federal fiscal policy in the early 1980s seemed aimed at providing a large counter-cyclical element into the economy so as to soften the impact of the 1982/83 recession. It was only beginning in 1986 that the federal government began to take discretionary actions to reduce its deficit and thus slow the rate of debt accumulation. Unfortunately, by 1986, the recession at the beginning of the decade, followed by a series of policy-induced increases in the deficit, had combined to almost double the debt/GDP ratio from 26% in 1980 to 50% by 1986.

By the end of the 1980s, debt servicing costs had become a major expenditure item for the federal government. By 1989, servicing the outstanding debt required an expenditure equal to 5.7% of GDP. The growth of the debt during the 1980s, and the consequent growth in debt servicing costs, was the sole reason for an average deficit over that period of 4.5% of GDP. If not for debt servicing costs, the federal budget would, on average, have been balanced during the 1980s. As it was, funds were being borrowed to pay all of the interest owed on funds borrowed previously.

The beginning of the 1990s saw the federal budget approaching a kind of delicate balance. The primary balance was in surplus so that in 1990 tax revenue exceeded program expenditures by 2.5% of GDP. The cost of servicing debt, however, was equal to 5.7% of GDP. Thus, although growth in the primary surplus was making headway against debt servicing costs, funds were still being borrowed to pay about half the cost of servicing outstanding debt. This, plus the fact the difference in the interest rate paid on federal debt and the rate of output growth had narrowed during the late 1980s, meant that growth in the debt/GDP ratio had slowed and was seemingly approaching a landing at about 55% of GDP.

The precarious nature of the federal government's finances was exposed in 1990 when the Bank of Canada, in an effort to achieve its target of zero inflation, drove interest rates upward. This in turn contributed to a major slowdown in economic growth. The stage was thus set for another rapid run-up in federal debt; the interest raid paid on federal debt now exceeded the rate of GDP growth by a wide margin, and, via its impact on automatic stabilizers, the recession would produce a primary deficit. The federal debt/GDP ratio quickly increased from 55% in 1990 to 71% by 1994.

Under these economic conditions, the debt/GDP ratio could only be prevented from increasing if the federal government introduced discretionary fiscal policy changes to dramatically increase the size of the primary surplus. As we will see in Chapter 4, such decisive action did not take place until 1994. The years 1994-98 saw the federal government introduce fiscal policies that increased its primary surplus to almost 5% of GDP by 1998. This had the effect of reducing the overall deficit from almost 6% of GDP in 1994 to zero by 1998. The effect was to again halt the growth of the debt/GDP ratio, this time at 70% of GDP.

During the 1960s, the fiscal history of the provinces was similar to that of the federal government. Budget deficits were typically small and often followed by surpluses. As evidenced by the small debt service figures in Table 2-5, provincial debts were also small. Notable exceptions were Newfoundland and PEI. Throughout the 1960s, Newfoundland ran very large deficits averaging 4.4% of GDP. Primary deficits were also large and indeed growing throughout the decade. By 1969, debt servicing costs had increased by more than three times from 0.8% to 2.6% of GDP. Although on average PEI ran more modest deficits, six of the nine years during this period gave rise to deficits, four of which were well in excess of 3% of GDP. In the last two years of the decade, PEI responded forcibly to the increase in its debt caused by the large deficits during the earlier part of the decade by running substantial primary surpluses. Over the next four years (1969-1972) PEI would run primary surpluses averaging in excess of 5.2% of GDP; doing so enabled it to dramatically reduce its debt/GDP ratio by mid-decade. This effort was aided, of course, by the combination of a high growth rate and relatively low interest rate.

The 1970s did not yield dramatic changes in the financial conditions of most of the provinces. For the most part, budget imbalances, both positive and negative, remained small. Exceptions were Alberta and Saskatchewan both of which enjoyed large primary surpluses thanks to increases in oil and gas prices. As a result, these provinces were able to significantly improve their net asset positions over the course of the decade. Another exception was Newfoundland which continued to run large deficits and which continued to pay the price in the form of a large and growing debt service. In 1974 Newfoundland paid another price for its large deficits when Moody's bond rating service lowered its credit rating to Baa1; a rating granted bonds which Moody's describes as "lack(ing) outstanding investment characteristics and in fact have speculative characteristics as well". Only in 1977 did Newfoundland implement a change in its fiscal philosophy and begin to budget substantial primary surpluses.

When interest rates soared in the early 1980s, with the consequent effect of slowing the rate of economic growth, the provinces found themselves in the same position as the federal government; the recession caused tax revenues to fall, expenditures to increase, and their primary deficits to grow. In conjunction with the unfavourable combination of a high interest rate and a low rate of economic growth, this was a recipe for high deficits and a rapid growth in debt/GDP ratios. The situation was most acute for provinces east of Ontario since they began the 1980s with relatively large debt/GDP ratios. Debt servicing costs already made up a large share of total expenditures in these provinces and a rise in interest rates would increase this expenditure item even further. Provinces west of Ontario began the decade either with small debt/GDP ratios (Manitoba) or were in net asset positions (Saskatchewan, Alberta and British Columbia). Thus the rise in interest rates and the economic slowdown, while a problem for all governments, was especially devastating for the provinces east of Ontario.

While Alberta and Saskatchewan had the advantage of being in net asset positions beginning the 1980s, they had to deal with collapsing commodity prices. Saskatchewan's finances suffered from the fall in oil and gas prices in 1986, and from low potash, uranium and grain prices throughout the decade. Saskatchewan moved from a net asset to a net debt position by 1985/86 and experienced a 24 percentage point worsening of its net debt position over the course of the decade. This prompted a series of credit downgrades that pushed up borrowing costs for the province. The collapse in oil prices also seriously affected Alberta's finances and caused Alberta to suffer a dramatic reduction in its net asset position – a 14 percentage point reduction in its asset/GDP ratio in only four years.

British Columbia dealt with the volatility of economic conditions during the 1980s by simply avoiding deficits. In non-recession years, British Columbia ran both deficits and surplus but neither ever exceeded 1% of GDP. As a consequence, although it too suffered the revenue loss due to the fall in energy prices and consequently an increase in its debt/GDP ratio following 1986, it managed to quickly reduce this ratio to near zero by the end of the decade. Large primary surpluses were not required in British Columbia during the 1980s due to its having entered the decade in a net asset position, and because large deficits were avoided. In this way, British Columbia was able to minimize the debilitating effects on its finances wrought by high interest rates.

Ontario's experience was much like British Columbia's in that its deficit/GDP ratio never exceeded 1% (either positive or negative) except during years of recession; in 1982 and 1983 Ontario's deficit peaked at 2% of GDP. Relatively small deficits, combined with a small debt/GDP ratio at the beginning of the decade that helped protect it from the effects of the period's high interest rates, enabled Ontario to leave the 1980s with its debt/GDP ratio at virtually the same level as it was at the beginning of the decade.

The return to high interest rates and slower economic growth in the early 1990s – and the consequent widening of the gap between interest rates and growth rates – would wreak havoc on provincial finances just as they did on federal finances. As Table 2-6 shows, many provinces saw their debt/GDP ratios double (or more) in the first few years of the 1990s.

Part of the explanation for this is surely attributable to the effects of a higher interest rate being paid on a large outstanding debt. Thus a province like Newfoundland, with a high debt/GDP ratio, would have difficulty preventing that ratio from rising still further in the face of increases in interest rates. On the other hand, a province like Ontario, with a low debt/GDP ratio, would have an easier time controlling growth in its debt. Interestingly, however, Table 2-6 shows that during the 1990s, the debt/GDP ratio grew very quickly in Ontario. The explanation for this must lie in what happened to Ontario's primary deficit. As Table 2-5 shows, Ontario moved from an average primary *surplus* of 1.2% of GDP during the 1980s to an average primary *deficit* of 0.2% of GDP in the 1990s. Part of this was certainly due to the effects of recession. However, while Ontario was not the only province affected by recession, it was the only province to allow its primary balance to move into deficit during this period. This suggests policy changes in tax rates and/or spending programs may also have played an important role, a conjecture we will show to be true in Chapter 4.

By 1998, the federal government and most of the provinces had established a set of tax rates and spending commitments that would yield a balanced budget or a budget surplus. Notable exceptions are Ontario and Quebec which continue to run deficits. But even these provinces have plans in place for reaching balanced budgets in the near future. Falling interest rates and improving prospects for economic growth have again narrowed the gap between these values so that economic conditions are favourable to maintaining a constant debt/GDP ratio. A factor crucial for determining whether, and how quickly, debt/GDP ratios will decline in the coming years is how the federal and provincial governments choose to respond to what is expected to be growing primary surpluses. If they choose to cut tax rates and/or increase program spending, the expected surpluses will either not materialize or will be smaller than otherwise. If so, debt/GDP ratios will either not shrink or will grow smaller less quickly than otherwise. In other words, the future direction of the debt/GDP ratios depend in large part on fiscal policy choices. In the next chapter, we provide some information on what these choices might have to be in order to meet certain targets. In Chapter 4, we will provide information on the choices that Canadian federal and provincial governments have made in the past. Both chapters, then, provide some clues to what the federal and provincial governments may choose to do in the future.

CHAPTER THREE

THE SUSTAINABILITY OF
FISCAL POLICY IN CANADA

The typical approach to comparing the fiscal stances of governments is to present comparative figures on revenues, program expenditures, net debt, and so forth, all expressed as a proportion of provincial GDP, or perhaps on a real per capita basis. This was the approach we took in Chapter 2.

While such comparisons are useful, they are lacking in an important respect – they say little about the *sustainability* of a government's fiscal stance. Comparisons that ignore whether or not a current fiscal stance is sustainable say nothing about whether or not the government will be forced to change its stance in the future. In this section, we address this issue by reporting a simple and intuitive measure of the sustainability of the fiscal stances adopted by both the federal and provincial governments.

What exactly do we mean by the sustainability of a government's fiscal policy? Olivier Blanchard suggests the following approach.[1] He defines a fiscal stance as sustainable if tax and expenditure settings are such that there will be no change in the net debt/GDP ratio over the horizon under consideration.

There are several ways of using this idea of sustainability to compare fiscal policies across provinces and the federal government at both a particular point in time and over time. The approach taken here, and suggested by Blanchard, is to suppose that the government's current program spending as a percentage of GDP is treated as given. This is to say, let's presume that the government wants to maintain its current program spending relative to the size of the economy. Now ask the following question: what is the tax/GDP ratio, which we refer to as the *sustainable tax rate*, that, given expectations regarding the interest rate on government debt, the growth rate in GDP, and the variance in that growth rate, will hold the current net debt/GDP ratio constant over the relevant horizon? In other words, what is the tax rate required to maintain the current program spending rate without causing the net debt/GDP ratio to either rise or fall?

This notion of fiscal sustainability is very useful, because it allows us to compare "apples to apples" when assessing the relative fiscal stances of the various provinces and the federal government. Comparing the level of sustainable tax rates across provinces, for example, is more meaningful than comparing what may be unsustainable current levels of tax revenue to GDP (what we call *actual* tax rates). Moreover, the *difference* between the sustainable and actual tax rate – the *tax gap* – provides a measure of possible changes to come. According to Blanchard (page 13), the tax gap tells us whether or not "given the current fiscal stance there will be a need for a drastic readjustment and, if so, of what magnitude." Finally, by looking at the difference between actual and sustainable tax rates over time, we are able to determine at which point in time each government moved to a sustainable, or an unsustainable, fiscal policy.

While we focus here on the presentation of *sustainable tax rates*, it is clear that we could also compute *sustainable expenditure rates* – i.e., given current taxes as a percentage of GDP, what ratio of program spending to GDP would be required to maintain the current debt/GDP ratio? Our focus on tax rates is arbitrary, and is not meant to suggest that adjusting tax rather than spending rates to achieve sustainability is the preferred approach.

3.1 Methodology

The above discussion has been somewhat general. It is now time to become more precise regarding what we mean by a sustainable tax rate. We extend Blanchard's approach in two ways. First, we account for the fact that an important source of revenues for many provinces is federal transfers. Second, unlike Blanchard, we explicitly account for the volatility of the economy in the form of uncertainty regarding the growth rate in GDP. While in his discussion Blanchard clearly has in mind the evaluation of fiscal policy in an uncertain environment, his formal derivations take place in a deterministic setting.

The starting point for our discussion of sustainability is the simple arithmetic of the government budget constraint introduced in Chapter 2. Here we present a slightly different version, but the basic idea is the same. The following representation of the government budget constraint provides the basis for our measure of sustainability:[2]

$$\Delta b = g - t - f + (r - y + \emptyset^2)b \qquad (3.1)$$

where, as in equation (2.1) in Chapter 2, Δb is the change in the net debt/GDP ratio over the coming year; g is program spending (total expenditures less interest paid on debt) relative to GDP; r is the interest rate;

and y is the rate of growth in GDP. There are two noteworthy differences between this equation and equation (2.1). The first involves the terms t and f. When analysing the sustainability of provincial fiscal policy, it is important to distinguish between own source revenue and transfers from the federal government (as discussed in Chapter 2, federal transfers are an important source of revenue for the provinces). For purposes of ascertaining the sustainability of provincial fiscal policy, we are interested in the province's *own source* tax revenue, which is tax revenue net of federal transfers. Thus, when equation (3.1) is applied to a province, t represents its own source taxes as a percentage of GDP, while f is federal transfers to that province relative to GDP. When we examine the sustainability of the federal fiscal stance, f is of course zero and t takes on the usual interpretation. The second noteworthy difference between the above equation and the earlier representation in Chapter 2 is the inclusion of the term ϕ^2, which is defined as the variance in the growth rate in GDP. This term will be discussed in more detail below.

As discussed, a fiscal stance is sustainable if the net debt/GDP ratio is not expected to change over time. Setting $\Delta b = 0$ in equation (3.1), and solving for t, gives the following measure of the sustainable tax rate:

$$t^* = g - f + (r - y + \phi^2)b \qquad (3.2)$$

Equation (3.2) is quite intuitive. Ignore for the moment the term representing the variance in GDP growth (ϕ^2). In order to maintain existing program spending as a proportion of GDP (g) and keep the net debt/GDP ratio from changing, own source revenues as a percentage of GDP (the sustainable tax rate t^*) must cover program spending not financed by federal transfers (the amount $g - f$) plus debt service costs (rb). Thus, the higher is program spending not financed by transfers and the higher is the cost of debt service, the higher is the sustainable tax rate. As discussed in Chapter 2, the term yb reflects the fact that the higher the growth rate in GDP, the lower the tax rate required to maintain the debt/GDP ratio at its current level.

The term $\phi^2 b$ in equation (3.2) requires some explanation; it is not included in Blanchard's original formulation of the sustainable tax rate nor in our earlier discussion of the government budget constraint in Chapter 2. Its presence in equation (3.2) suggests that the greater the variability in provincial GDP, the higher is the sustainable tax rate. To see why this is the case, note first that if we intend to use (3.1) and (3.2) to determine what sustainable tax rate government should set for the coming year, then each element in these equations should be interpreted as an expected value. Thus, Δb is the *expected* change in the debt/GDP ratio over the coming year, and t, g and f are *expected* own source tax revenues, program spending and federal transfers relative to GDP over the year.

Second, note that the debt/GDP ratio, $b=B/GDP$, is a non-linear function of GDP. In particular, for a given stock of debt, b is decreasing in *GDP* at a decreasing rate, as depicted in Figure 3-1. To see the implications of this, say that the current debt/GDP ratio is b_0 and GDP is GDP_0. Now suppose that over the next period, GDP is *expected* to remain at the current level (i.e., the expected rate of growth is zero), but that there is a 50% chance that it will increase by ΔGDP to GDP_H, and a 50% chance that it will decrease by (the same) ΔGDP to GDP_L. If GDP rises to GDP_H, then b_0 will fall to b_L and if GDP falls to GDP_L then b_0 will rise to b_H. Because b is decreasing in GDP at a decreasing rate, the rise in b due to a fall in GDP is greater than the fall in b due to a rise in GDP of the same magnitude. Thus, although the *expected* rate of growth in GDP is zero, the debt/GDP ratio is *expected* to rise to b'. The greater the volatility in GDP – i.e., the greater is ΔGDP – the higher is the expected increase in the debt/GDP ratio, all else equal. In order to offset this, the sustainable tax rate must be higher. Thus, we get the rather interesting insight that, all else being equal, a province with a more volatile economy will require a higher tax rate relative to GDP in order to maintain its program spending and current level of debt.

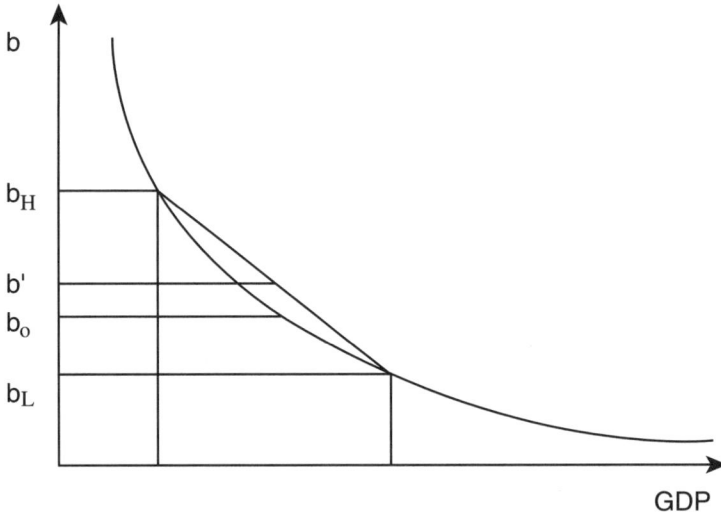

Given the definition of the sustainable tax rate in equation (3.2), we can determine whether existing fiscal policy is sustainable by comparing the sustainable tax rate, t^*, to the actual tax rate, t. If the tax gap, $t^* - t$, is positive – i.e., the sustainable tax rate exceeds the actual tax rate – then the current fiscal policy stance of the government is not sustainable in the sense that the net debt/GDP ratio will be expected to increase unless changes are made to either tax or spending policy. On the other hand, if the tax gap is negative, then, by our definition, the current fiscal policy stance is also not sustainable in the sense that the net debt/GDP ratio will be expected to decrease over the coming year unless changes are made to either tax or spending policy. Thus, the tax gap tells us what fiscal adjustment is required in order to maintain the current debt/GDP ratio.

It should be stressed that the definition of sustainability says nothing about the optimality, or appropriateness, of fiscal policy. It may well be a good policy decision to allow the net debt/GDP ratio to rise or fall over some period of time. Thus, good fiscal policy may well involve running fiscal policy that is not sustainable by our definition for an extended period of time as the government moves to a new debt/GDP ratio. For example, with high levels of debt, governments may well want to run non-sustainable fiscal policies that reduce the debt/GDP ratio over time. We will return to this issue in our discussion of the calculations later in this chapter.

With equations (3.1) and (3.2) in hand, we have a graphic illustration of the familiar TNSTAAFL principle in economics – "there's no such thing as a free lunch." A fiscal stance involving high expenditure rates (g), low tax rates (t), large deficits and therefore a growing debt/GDP ratio (b) is unsustainable. Debt/GDP cannot grow forever, because eventually the debt service costs (rb) will outgrow the ability of the economy to finance them. Moreover, past indiscretions, as represented by a high current debt/GDP ratio, must eventually manifest themselves in a high tax rate (or low expenditure rate) if fiscal policy is to be put back on a sustainable course. As discussed in Chapter 2, this also leaves the economy exposed to increases in the interest rate (r), which increase debt service costs (rb), and if persistent, must be met with either an increase in the tax rate (t) or decrease in the spending rate (g) if fiscal policy is to become sustainable again. It is thus important to identify systematically unsustainable fiscal policies early on. Moreover, the equations also highlight the important role played by economic growth and the volatility in that growth.

Contrary to popular belief, sustainable fiscal policy does not require that the government run a balanced budget, even over the business cycle. To see this, simply rearrange equation (3.2) to solve for the *sustainable deficit* (expressed relative to GDP):

$$d^* = (g - t - f + rb)^* = (y - \phi^2)b \qquad (3.3)$$

This is the deficit/GDP ratio that is expected to maintain the existing net debt/GDP ratio. As long as $d \le (y - \phi^2)b$, the debt/GDP ratio will not be expected to grow over time (and indeed if $d < (y - \phi^2)b$, will in fact be expected to shrink). Thus, high expected growth (y), and/or low volatility (ϕ^2), will allow the government to run a higher (sustainable) deficit.

Note, however, that in the presence of net debt, sustainability may preclude the government from running a *primary* deficit, and may indeed require the presence of a primary surplus. This means that the government must collect more in revenues than it spends on government programs net of interest payments. This can be seen by once again rearranging equation (3.2) to solve for the *sustainable primary deficit* (again expressed relative to GDP):

$$pd^* = (g - t - f)^* = - (r - y + \emptyset^2)b \qquad (3.4)$$

where pd^* is the sustainable primary deficit. If $r > y + \emptyset^2$, then pd^* is negative, i.e., a primary *surplus* is in fact required for sustainability. As we saw in Chapter 2, the interest rate has exceeded the GDP growth rate in Canada since the early 1980s. Including the variance in GDP growth as above would simply increase the gap. This suggests that since the early1980s, in the presence of a (sizable) net debt, governments in Canada have needed to run primary surpluses for sustainability.

Before turning to our calculations, we must emphasize two very important points regarding how the sustainability numbers that follow should be interpreted. The first is to re-emphasize that sustainability should not be mistaken for optimality. The appropriate fiscal stance may well be to run non-sustainable policy over a period of time as the government moves towards a new debt/GDP ratio. As such, a persistently positive or negative tax gap should not be construed in and of itself as either a good or a bad thing, but rather as indicative of a change in the fiscal direction of the government in question. The specific circumstances must be taken into account.

Second, as presented above, the government budget constraint from which the sustainability conditions are derived (equation (3.1)) is a forward looking condition. It describes the expected change in the net debt/GDP ratio given expectations about GDP growth, interest rates, and tax and spending rates. This raises the issue of the use of government forecasts and the time horizon used to make those forecasts. Blanchard recommends two types of tax gap calculations, depending upon the time horizon. *Primary tax gaps* are short term, and use actual tax and spending rates calculated over the year, as well as current, or actual, interest and growth rates (or possibly a moving average). *Medium-term tax gaps* use medium term forecasts of these variables typically included in budget documents. The problem with primary tax gaps is that they accentuate short-term fluctuations in tax and expenditure rates due to economic fluctuations associated with the business cycle (an issue that will be revisited in Chapter 4). The problem with medium-term tax gaps is that they are based upon forecasts contained in budgets. As discussed in Chapter 1, we have chosen to use FMS data for most of the analysis in this volume, because of its consistency over time and across provinces. This means that we must work with realized data rather than forecasts, and therefore that we are restricted to primary tax gap and sustainability calculations. While we experimented with various smoothing techniques to deal with fluctuations due to the business cycle, they did not materially affect the results; so we stuck with the simple primary gap calculations. Because there is a tendency for our primary gap calculations to vary according to economic conditions, when comparing tax gaps over time we should pay attention not so much as to whether they are positive or negative, or whether they are high or low in a particular year, but rather to the general trend in the tax gap. We are looking for persistently positive or negative primary tax gaps over time, and particularly over business cycles, as an indication of the direction of fiscal policy. We will return to this issue below in our discussion of the results, to which we now turn.

3.2 Tax Gaps and Sustainability: The Calculations

As discussed previously, program spending, federal transfers, debt service costs, and own source revenues are based upon 1996 FMS data, which includes the most recent comparable provincial figures. Program spending is simply total provincial expenditures (current and capital) less debt service costs. Federal transfers include Established Program Financing (EPF), Canada Assistance Plan (CAP) payments, the Canada Health and Social Transfer (CHST), where appropriate, and equalization payments. Net debt for each province is measured as the difference between gross financial liabilities and financial assets.

Figures 3-1 to 3-12 illustrate our calculations of the primary tax gap, t^* - t, and the net debt/GDP ratio for the federal government, all provinces aggregated together, and each individual province from 1977 to 1996.[3] In these diagrams the tax gap uses the left scale of the diagram while the net debt/GDP ratio uses the right scale. Note in particular that each scale has a different origin.

We begin with a discussion of the sustainability of federal fiscal policy over the period. From Figure 3-2, we note first that, as discussed earlier, the federal primary tax gap has indeed been somewhat cyclical, with the gap increasing with the 1981/82 recession, falling off after that, and repeating this cycle with the 1990/91 recession. However, although there have been some fluctuations throughout the period, it is important to note that the federal tax gap was persistently positive throughout the period from 1977 to 1995. Although it dropped off (eventually) following the recessions, it stayed positive nonetheless. This is, of course, indicative of a long term fiscal sustainability problem, as reflected in the rising net debt/GDP ratio throughout the period. Net debt as a percentage of GDP increased from about 15% in 1977 and reached a high of 72% in 1995. The tax gap over

Figure 3-2 Tax Gap and Net Debt: Federal Government

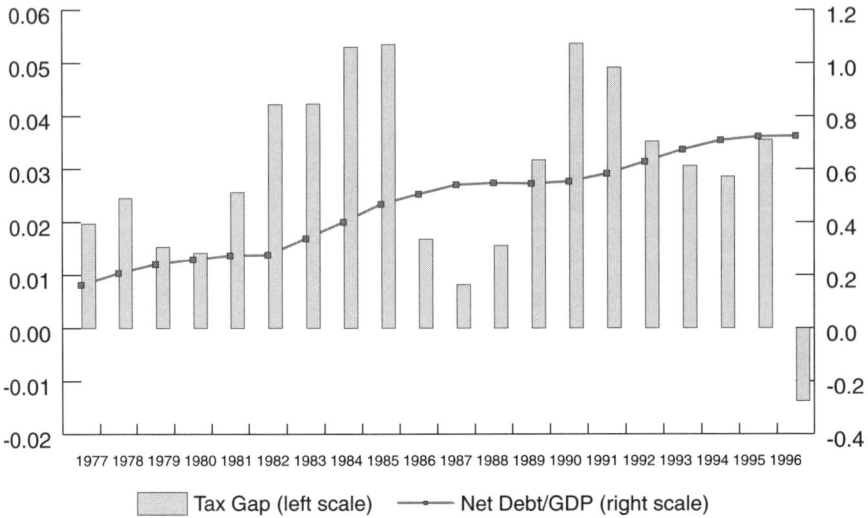

Tax Gap (left scale) ——— Net Debt/GDP (right scale)

this period ranged from less than one percentage point in 1987 to around five percentage points in 1984 and 1985, and 1990 and 1991. The rate of growth in the net debt/GDP ratio has closely followed these fluctuations, with a sharp increase starting in the early eighties when the tax gap broad-

Figure 3-3 Tax Gap and Net Debt: Aggregate Provincial Governments

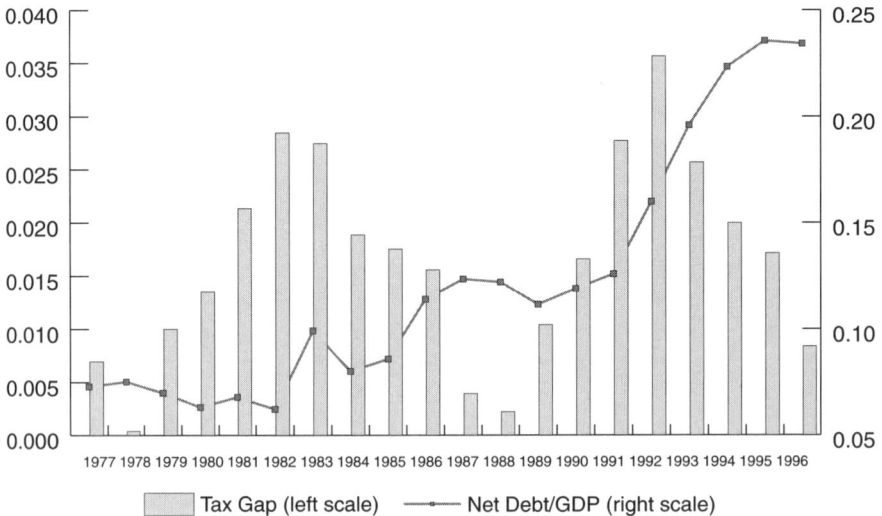

Tax Gap (left scale) ——— Net Debt/GDP (right scale)

Figure 3-4 Tax Gap and Net Debt: British Columbia

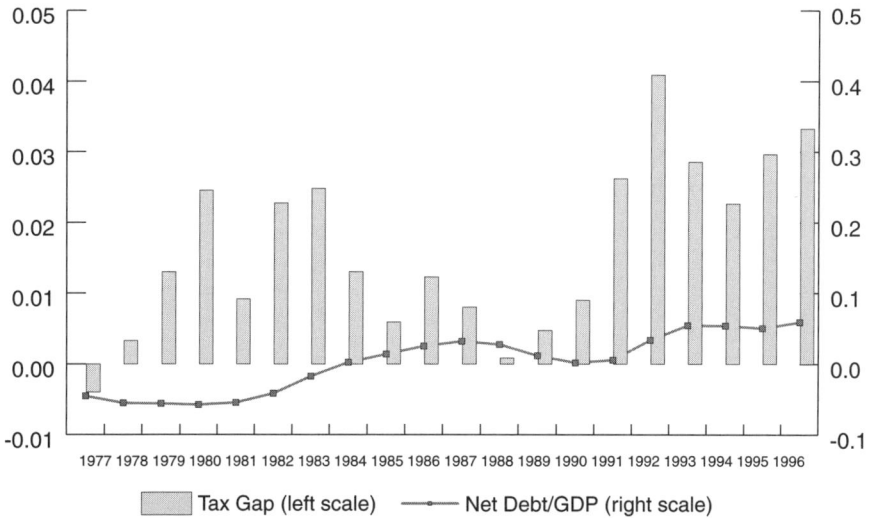

Tax Gap (left scale) ——— Net Debt/GDP (right scale)

ened substantially, slowing down slightly in the late eighties as the gap narrowed, and then picking up again in the early nineties as the gap once again widened. The average gap over the period from 1977 to 1995 was about three percentage points. This means that in order to have maintained program spending and stabilize the debt/GDP ratio, the average federal tax rate (taxes/GDP) would have had to have been higher by about

Figure 3-5 Tax Gap and Net Debt: Alberta

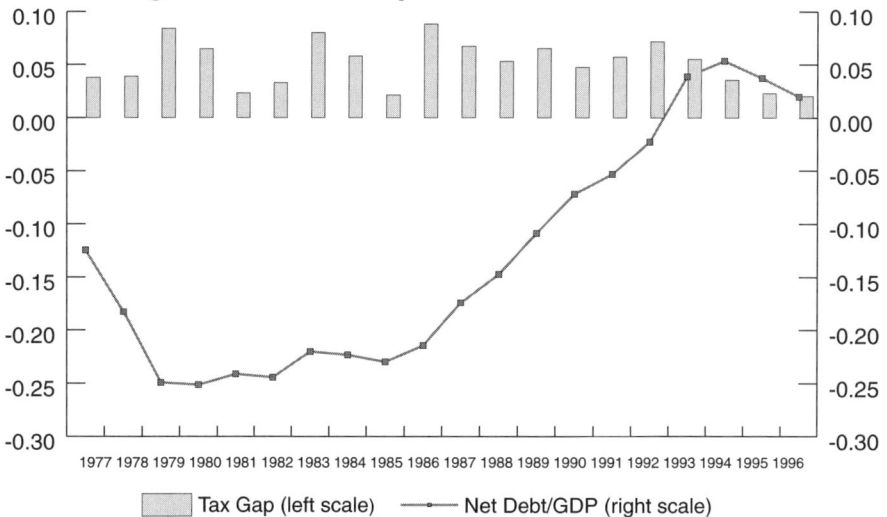

Tax Gap (left scale) ——— Net Debt/GDP (right scale)

Figure 3-6 Tax Gap and Net Debt: Saskatchewan

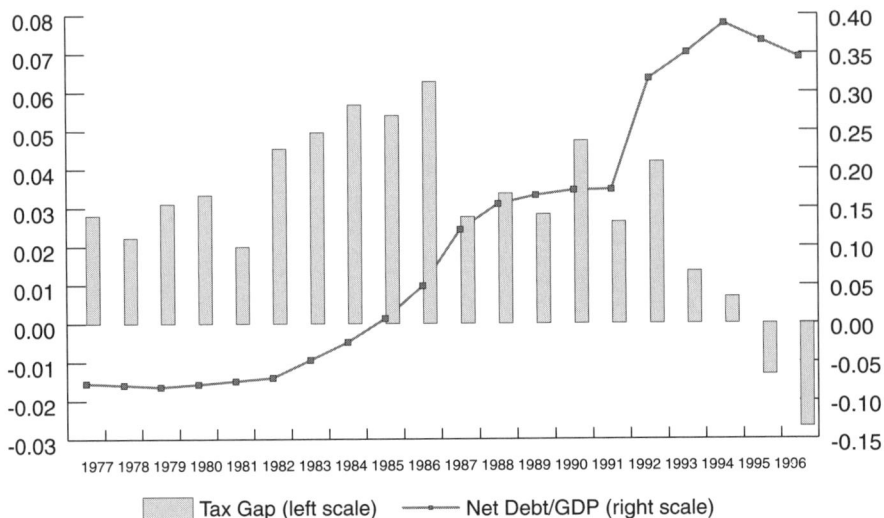

Tax Gap (left scale)   ——— Net Debt/GDP (right scale)

three percentage points; or, conversely, that program spending relative to GDP would have had to have been lower by about three percentage points. Particularly noteworthy from Figure 3-2 is the still positive tax gaps through the second half of the 1980s. This despite real output growth over that period of about 4%. The inability (or refusal) of the federal government to move to a negative tax gap over this period, and therefore to bring

Figure 3-7 Tax Gap and Net Debt: Manitoba

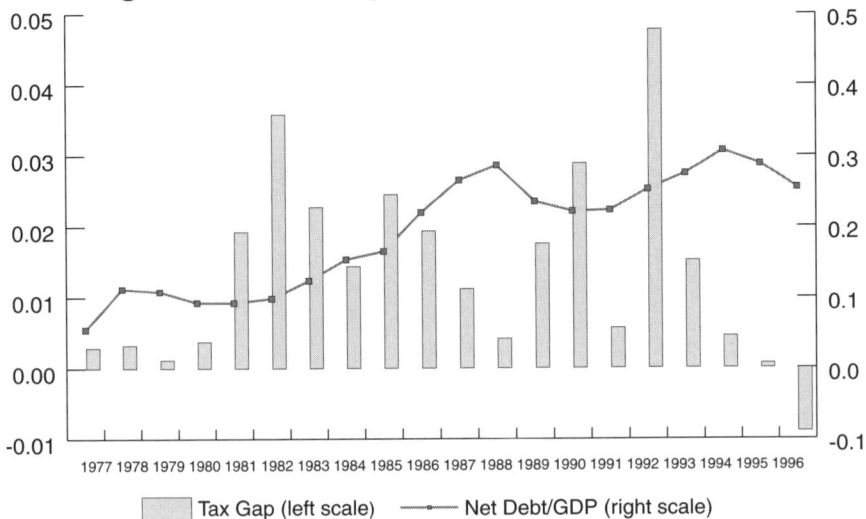

Tax Gap (left scale)   ——— Net Debt/GDP (right scale)

Figure 3-8 Tax Gap and Net Debt: Ontario

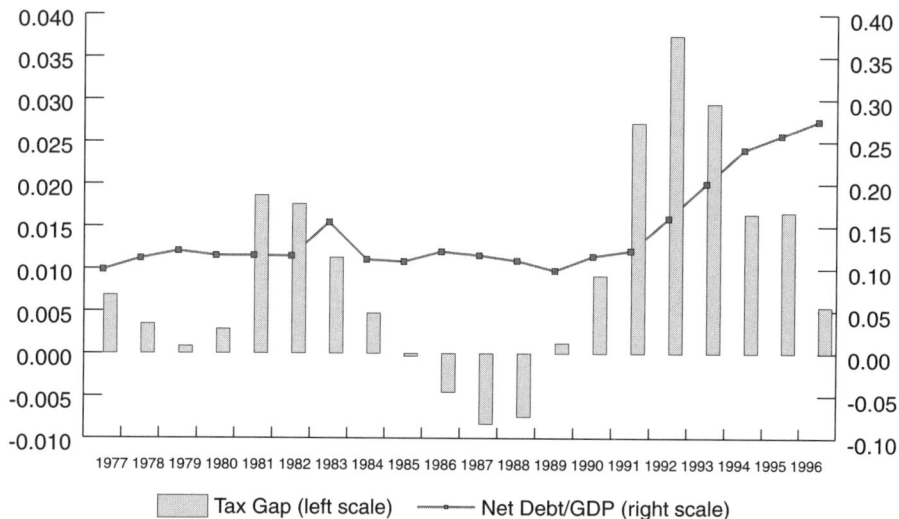

Tax Gap (left scale)   Net Debt/GDP (right scale)

down the debt/GDP ratio, laid the groundwork for a substantial run-up in the ratio following the 1990/91 recession.

Things changed in 1996. For the first time in twenty years, the federal tax gap turned negative, by about 1.4 percentage points of GDP. This amounted to just over $11 billion dollars – i.e., taxes could have been $11 billion lower or expenditures $11 billion higher (or some combination

Figure 3-9 Tax Gap and Net Debt: Quebec

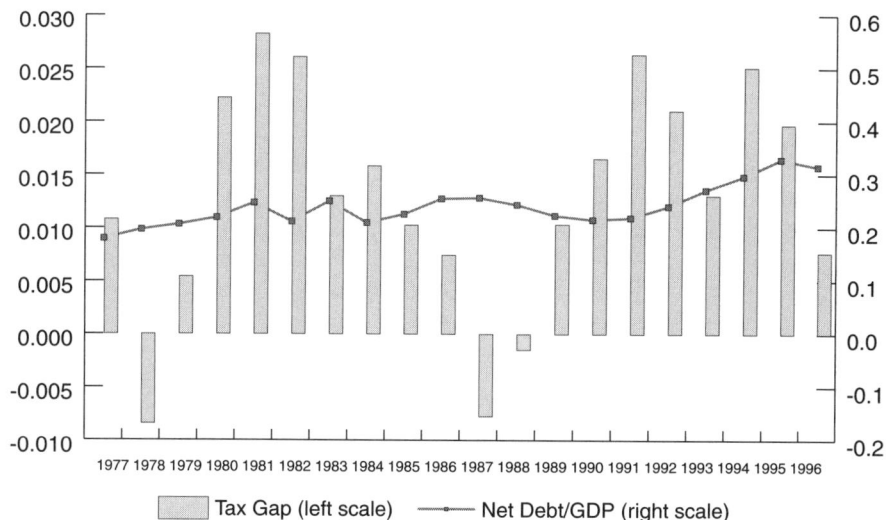

Tax Gap (left scale)   Net Debt/GDP (right scale)

Figure 3-10 Tax Gap and Net Debt: New Brunswick

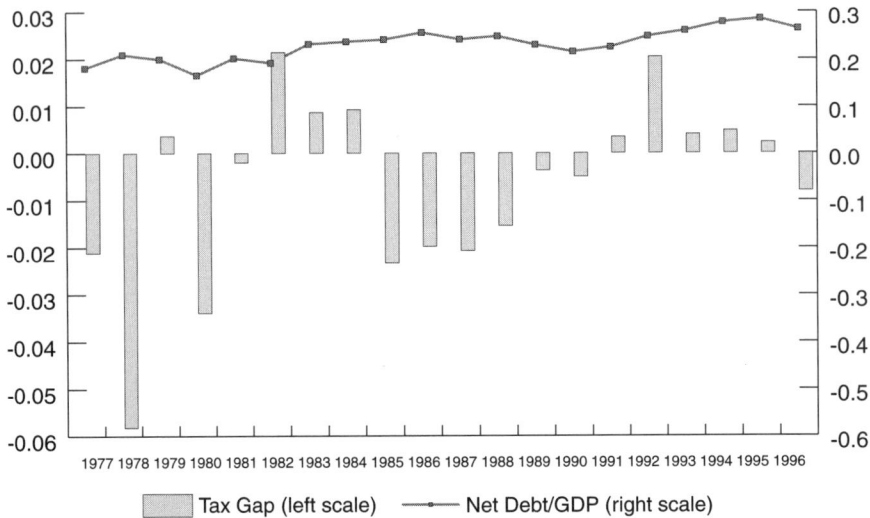

Tax Gap (left scale) ——■—— Net Debt/GDP (right scale)

thereof) in 1996 to maintain the debt/GDP ratio at the (very high!) level of 73%. As we would expect, this was accompanied by a substantial flattening out of the net debt/GDP ratio. Does this represent a turning point? On the basis of the historical FMS data underlying the calculations it is difficult to say. However, as the first negative tax gap in two decades it is definitely noteworthy. Moreover, as we know, the federal government has continued

Figure 3-11 Tax Gap and Net Debt: Nova Scotia

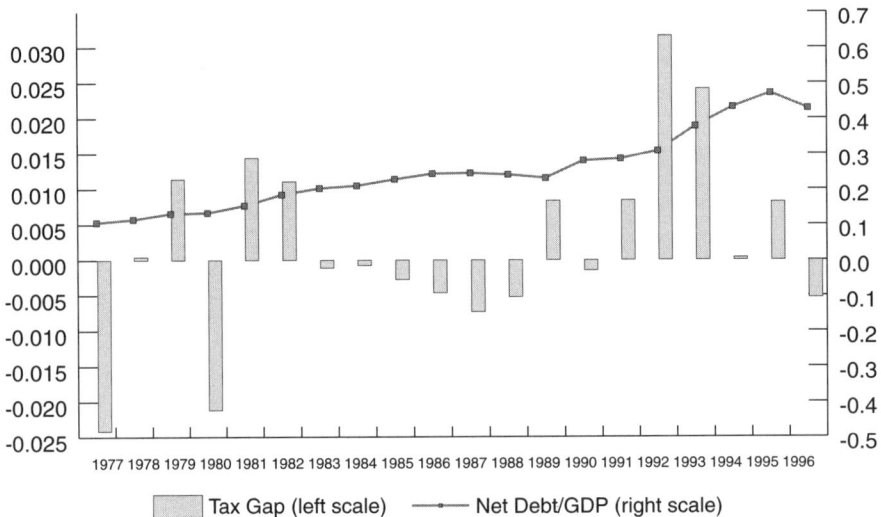

Tax Gap (left scale) ——■—— Net Debt/GDP (right scale)

Figure 3-12 Tax Gap and Net Debt: Prince Edward Island

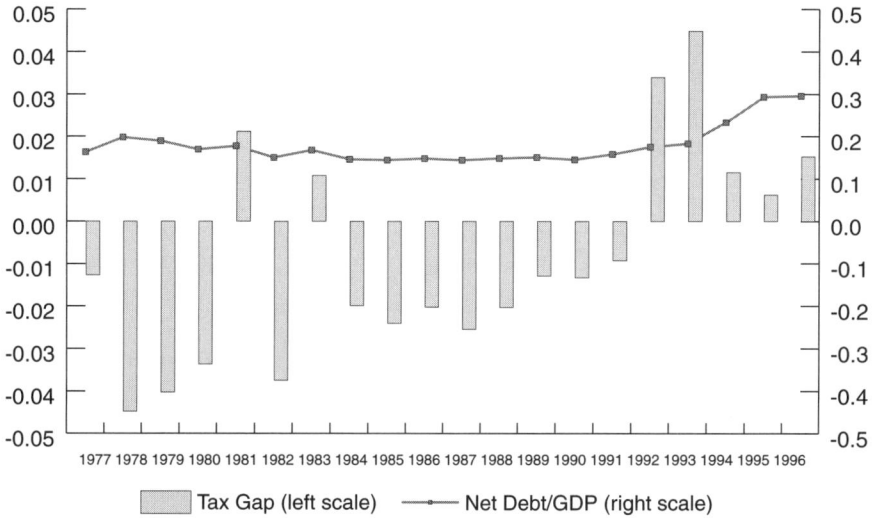

Tax Gap (left scale)   Net Debt/GDP (right scale)

on the fiscal course charted in 1996, having tabled its first surplus government in almost thirty years in 1998. Our expectation would be that the federal primary tax gap has remained negative, and possibly broadened somewhat, throughout 1997 and 1998. Of course to lower the net debt/GDP ratio, the federal government must continue to run persistently (and, by our definition, non-sustainable!) negative tax gaps for several years.

Figure 3-13 Tax Gap and Net Debt: Newfoundland

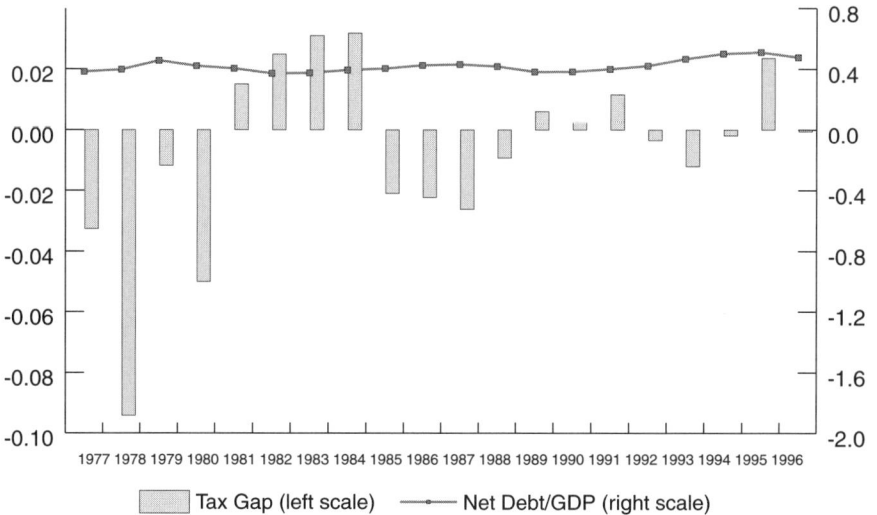

Tax Gap (left scale)   Net Debt/GDP (right scale)

An interesting question concerns the source of the narrowing federal tax gap in the 1990s. Table 3-1 decomposes the tax gap over the period 1990-1996 into some of its component parts. There are two declines in the gap that are noteworthy. The first was the drop in the tax gap that occurred from 1991 to 1992, from 4.9% to 3.5%. The gap then stayed steady between 2.8% and 3.5% for three years. The second was the change from a positive tax gap of 3.5% in 1995 to a negative gap of -1.4% in 1996 – an almost 5 percentage point turn around. What were the reasons for the narrowing of the gap in 1992 and again in 1996?

Dealing first with the 1.4 percentage point drop in 1992, note that the actual tax rate (t) was relatively constant throughout the 1990 to 1995 period (from 16.7% to 17.8%), as was the spending rate (g), at around 17%. However, the last column in Table 3-1 shows that combined changes in interest and growth rates subtracted about 1.5 percentage points from the sustainable tax rate from 1991 to 1992, which almost exactly matches the reduction in the tax gap. This suggests that the source of the narrowing of the federal tax gap in 1992 was due almost exclusively to a narrowing of the spread between the interest rate and the growth rate (plus volatility), which lowered the sustainable tax rate through its interaction with government debt. This was also illustrated in Figure 2-1 from Chapter 2. Thus, the decline in the tax gap from 1991 to 1992 was due largely to factors beyond the control of the federal government – low interest rates and strong economic growth. Of course, the federal government did play a role in building up the large debt/GDP ratio that made the impact of the reduced interest rate-growth rate spread all the more important, but we would not consider that a positive contribution!

The turn to a negative gap in 1996 occurred for different reasons. In 1996, there was a two percentage point rise in the actual tax rate, from 16.7% to 18.9%. Moreover, the spending rate also fell by a full percentage point (from 15.7% to 14.7%). Thus, just over 3 percentage points of the 4.5 percentage point turn around in the tax gap from 1995 to 1996 came from a rise in the tax rate and a decline in the spending rate. This was reflective, at least in part, of deliberate policy decisions on the part of the federal government. We will address this issue much more closely in Chapter 4 where we discuss discretionary versus non-discretionary policy changes.

While it would appear that the federal government turned the corner in 1996, the jury is still out on the provinces as a whole. Turning to the aggregate provincial tax gaps in Figure 3-3, we see a similar cyclical pattern to the federal case – tax gaps tend to grow going into recessions (as in 1981/82 and 1990/91) and then narrow coming out of recessions. But the key point, as with the federal government, is that the gaps remain persistently positive, as manifested in the growing net provincial

Table 3-1   The Federal Tax Gap: 1990-1996 (percent)

	Sustainable Tax Rate (t*)	Actual Tax Rate (t)	Tax Gap (t*-t)	Spending Rate (g)	$(r-y+\phi^2)b$
1990	22.0	16.7	5.4	16.0	6.0
1991	22.2	17.3	4.9	17.5	4.7
1992	21.3	17.8	3.5	17.9	3.5
1993	20.1	17.0	3.1	17.8	2.3
1994	19.6	16.7	2.8	16.5	3.1
1995	20.3	16.7	3.5	15.7	4.5
1996	17.5	18.9	-1.4	14.7	2.7

Source: Author calculations.

debt/GDP ratio throughout the period. As a group, although there are signs that the provinces are moving towards a more sustainable fiscal policy with the narrowing of the tax gap in 1996, the gap is still positive, which suggests that the aggregate net provincial debt/GDP ratio is poised to continue the growth that has taken place throughout the period. This is because, as we shall see, as of 1996 some of Canada's largest provinces still had not adopted a fiscal position consistent with a declining debt/GDP ratio.

Figure 3-4 shows that British Columbia is one of the main culprits in this regard. With net debt that is only 6% of GDP in 1996, British Columbia is hardly in a fiscal straight-jacket. However, there are signs that the province may be headed for trouble. By running persistently positive tax gaps from 1978 through 1996, British Columbia has managed to turn a 5% net asset position in 1977 into a 6% net debt position by 1996; an eleven percentage point turnaround. Moreover, much of this has occurred since 1990. The tax gap in British Columbia from 1990 to 1996 has averaged 2.7 percentage points, and at almost 3.5 percentage points in 1996 there is no indication that it is poised for a decline. Given current (1996) economic conditions, in order to maintain the net debt/GDP ratio at the 6% level in 1996, B.C. would need to increase taxes or decrease expenditures by about $3.7 billion.

From Figure 3-8 we see that much of the growth in the net debt/GDP ratio in Ontario has occurred in the 1990s as well. Not surprisingly, this coincided with the emergence of sizeable positive tax gaps in Ontario. The sustainable tax rate exceeded the actual tax rate by almost four percentage points in 1992. While the tax gap has fallen off slightly since then, to only about 0.5 percentage points in 1996, it is still positive nonetheless. However, there are signs that starting in 1996 Ontario is at least approaching a fiscal stance consistent with non-increasing debt/GDP, as the tax gap has narrowed. Nonetheless, the fiscal policy in 1996 was still not consistent with a stable net debt/GDP ratio – as of 1996 sustainability still requires tax increases or expenditure cuts of about $1.6 billion. As we will discuss in more detail in the next chapter, the widening of the tax gap in the early 1990s coincided with the Bob Rae NDP government in Ontario, while the recent narrowing coincides with the Mike Harris Progressive Conservatives coming to power.

In Quebec, as well, we see some early signs in 1996 that the fiscal stance may have turned, but, as with Ontario and British Columbia, we see tax gaps that ebb and flow with the business cycle while generally remaining positive throughout the period.

Alberta is an interesting case, as we do not see the same cycles as we do in the country as a whole or in the other larger provinces (see Figure 3-5). Also notable in Alberta are the persistently positive, and large, tax gaps over the past twenty years. While in 1996 the province was in only a very slight net debt position, this marked a 25 percentage point turnaround that started with a net asset position of 25% of GDP in the late 1970s. The primary tax gap in Alberta has averaged over 5 percentage points throughout the period from 1977 to 1996, the largest of any of the provinces. While by starting in a deep net asset position the province could 'afford' such a non-sustainable fiscal stance throughout the period – and indeed this policy may well have been consistent with a sensible movement away from a net asset position to a low net debt/GDP ratio – it clearly can not go on forever. Since the election of the Ralph Klein Conservative government in 1992, and its first budget in 1993, the tax gap has steadily shrunk to its lowest level in twenty years, but it remains slightly positive as of 1996. Alberta's high, and unsustainable, tax gap over the past 20 years suggests that the perceived fiscal malaise the province found itself in in the early 1990s was born in the distant past, and is in many ways inconsistent with the typical view of Alberta as the bastion of fiscal conservatism. Nonetheless, the relatively quick action the province took in 1993, reflected in the substantial narrowing of the tax gap despite a still very low net debt/GDP ratio, may well be indicative of a lower tolerance for debt in Alberta relative to the rest of the country.

Some of the economically smaller provinces also offer some interesting case studies. Saskatchewan's net debt/GDP ratio grew from a slightly negative position to almost 40% by 1993 (see Figure 3-6). Such a large net debt position required fast and deep action to move to fiscal sustainability. The province initiated such actions in 1993 when the tax gap narrowed substantially. The gap turned negative, and the net debt/GDP ratio began falling, in 1995. In 1996 the actual tax rate in Saskatchewan exceeded the sustainable rate by almost three percentage points of GDP (about $8.4 million), suggesting a fiscal position solidly in favour of a decline in net debt/GDP. Similarly, Manitoba took drastic action in 1993 with a net debt/GDP ratio nearing 30%. The Atlantic provinces have also tended to move to fiscal sustainability more quickly and decisively than the economically larger provinces.

The lesson here seems to be that the smaller, less wealthy provinces tended to move to fiscally sustainable policies in the 1990s slightly ahead of, and more decisively than, the larger, wealthier provinces. This may have been due to the fact that they had little choice – with net debt/GDP ratios in excess, some well in excess, of 30%, these provinces were simply in no position to continue on their unsustainable paths. Some of the larger provinces, notably British Columbia and Alberta, still have comfortably low debt as a percentage of GDP, but the lessons of the smaller provinces should not be lost upon them – fiscal laxity now invites fiscal pain in the future, so says the simple arithmetic of government debt! This is a lesson that seems to have been learned in Alberta; British Columbia is another story. Ontario and Quebec have debt/GDP ratios more on par with some of the smaller provinces, but have chosen to move slowly nonetheless. Time will tell whether or not this will prove to be a sound policy.

What is interesting from our analysis of the tax gaps is that while most provinces and the federal government took decisive steps towards slowing, or reversing, the growth in debt/GDP ratios in the 1990s, they did so at very different debt/GDP ratios. The federal ratio was about 73% before we observe the first negative tax gap in many years. In Saskatchewan and most of the eastern provinces, debt/GDP ratios were in the neighbourhood of 40%. In Ontario and Quebec we still had not observed sustainable fiscal policy by 1996 at ratios of around 30%, while in Alberta decisive fiscal retrenchment occurred with virtually no net debt at all. British Columbia, with a net debt/GDP ratio of around 10%, has yet to take decisive action.

An intriguing question is why the various jurisdictions seemed to hit some sort of "fiscal wall", where a major fiscal retrenchment was deemed necessary, at very different levels of debt relative to the size of the economy – and remember, by looking at debt/GDP *ratios* we are already controlling for the size of the economy? It would seem that both the size and the location of the "fiscal wall" varies substantially across jurisdictions. While we will take up this question in more detail in the concluding chapter of the monograph (Chapter 6), one possible explanation may lie in the economic diversity and associated resiliency of the larger, wealthier provinces. This allows them, and the federal government, to handle a larger debt relative to the size of the economy than the smaller, less diverse provinces. This has, we think, some interesting implications for fiscal federalism, and the implications of the federal government downloading its deficit to the provinces via a reduction in transfers. We explore these implications in Chapter 6.

To conclude this chapter we turn, finally, to Figure 3-14, which presents a comparison of the sustainable tax rates across the provinces in 1996. The calculations illustrated in this figure are notable for a couple of reasons.

Figure 3-14 Total Sustainable Tax Rates: 1996

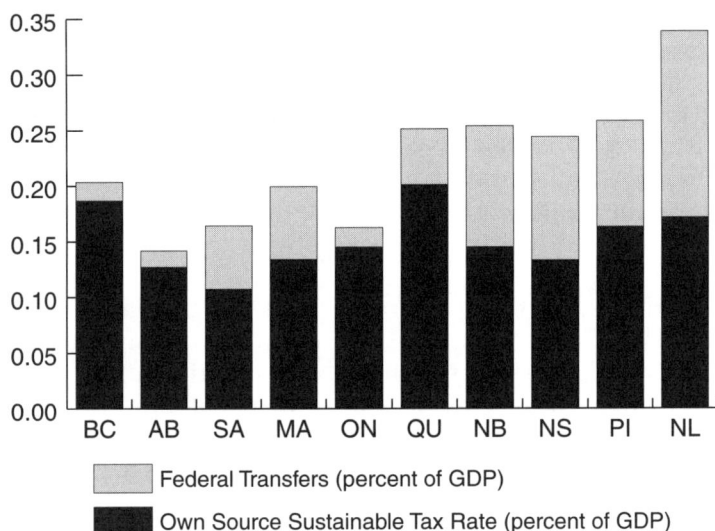

First, comparing the *own source* sustainable tax rates across the provinces says something about what we might think of as the *fiscal competitiveness* of the provinces. These are the own source tax rates required to maintain the existing net debt/GDP ratio given federal transfers and program expenditures. The figure is revealing in this regard. Note, for example, that the lowest own source sustainable tax rate is in Saskatchewan, at just over 11%. This may be somewhat surprising, but is suggestive of the fairly substantial cuts to government spending in Saskatchewan (as a percentage of GDP) initiated in the early 1990s. Next, perhaps less surpris-

PAST (IN)DISCRETIONS

ing, is Alberta, with an own source sustainable tax at around 12%. The highest own source sustainable tax rate is in Quebec, at about 20% – almost double the rate in Saskatchewan; British Columbia is close behind at about 19%. This is reflective of the relatively high spending rates in these provinces, and, in the case of Quebec, the high current net debt/GDP ratio. As mentioned above, neither province has initiated a movement toward a more competitive fiscal environment. Perhaps most surprising in the figure are the relatively low sustainable own source sustainable tax rates in the Atlantic provinces.

This brings us to the second issue of note from Figure 3-14. We have added to the own source sustainable tax rates federal transfers as a percentage of GDP. This serves two purposes. The first is to highlight the very large discrepancies in federal transfers across the provinces. The "have-not" Atlantic provinces are noteworthy beneficiaries of federal transfers, due largely to the equalization program. This should not be surprising. The second purpose is served by adding the federal transfer/GDP ratio to the own source sustainable tax rate. This tells us what the own source tax rate in each province would have to be in the absence of federal transfers in order to sustain current program spending as a percentage of GDP while maintaining a constant net debt/GDP ratio. The differences across the provinces is striking. In order to maintain its current spending and net debt/GDP ratio in the absence of federal transfers, Newfoundland would have to about double its own source tax rate to 35%. In Quebec the own source tax rate would have to increase by about 5 percentage points and in Saskatchewan by about 8 percentage points. Alberta has the lowest combined own source tax rate of just under 15%. This illustrates in rather striking fashion the role played by federal-provincial transfers in keeping the "have-not" provinces more fiscally competitive with the "have" provinces.

Appendix 3-1

The derivation of equation (3.1) in the text begins with an equation describing changes in the nominal stock of net debt,

$$dB = [G - F - T + rB]ds$$

We can write a stochastic equation of motion for GDP,

$$dGDP = GDPyds + GDP\emptyset dW$$

where B is the stock of net debt, G is total program expenditures, F is federal transfers, r the interest rate on government debt, y is the expected rate of growth in GDP, ø is the standard deviation in that growth rate, and dW the increment in a standard Weiner process with expected value of zero.

The net debt/GDP ratio is $b=B/GDP$. Utilizing Ito's Lemma to totally differentiate this with respect to B and GDP gives:

$$db = [g - f - t + (r - y + ø)]ds - bødW$$

Taking the expectation of this, remembering that $E[dW]=0$, and expressing the result per unit time, gives,

$$Es[^{db}/_{ds}] = g - t - f + (r - y + ø^2)b$$

which is equation (3.1) in the text.

CHAPTER FOUR

THE CHARACTERISTICS OF FISCAL POLICY IN CANADA

In this chapter, we examine in more detail some of the characteristics of the fiscal policy of provincial and federal governments. We begin by confronting an important issue that complicates the analysis of fiscal policy: to examine government budgetary *choices* we must first identify them. This is more difficult than it might at first appear because government budgets are influenced by both policy decisions and by economic conditions that are largely beyond the control of the government. Some revenue sources for the governments, such as personal income taxes, sales taxes, and the GST, are very sensitive to economic conditions, as are some expenditures, such as unemployment insurance and welfare. The sensitivity of revenues and expenditures to economic conditions results in what is commonly referred to as the "automatic stabilizing" feature of government budgets. When the economy grows slower than usual, government revenues are lower and expenditures are higher than usual. This increases the deficit, and provides a stimulus to the economy that moderates the reduction in the growth rate. When the economy grows faster than usual the opposite occurs, and the resulting decrease in the deficit dampens the growth in the economy. As such, income sensitive revenues and expenditures automatically help to stabilize the economy by reducing the amplitude of economic fluctuations. This has important implications for determining the fiscal policy stance of the government, as we must identify and distinguish between changes in revenues and expenditures due to economic fluctuations and changes due to fiscal policy choices. In particular, how much have deficits been reduced by automatic stabilizers versus discretionary policy choices? Olivier Blanchard helps us out again, and in this chapter we employ a method recently suggested by Blanchard to separate changes in federal and provincial government budget positions due to the business cycle from those arising from fiscal policy choices.[1]

Having identified changes in the budgetary stance in this way, we then investigate the *composition* of these various types of stances. Governments can reduce their budget deficits by cutting spending, by raising taxes, or by some combination of the two. In which of these ways have the various Canadian governments reduced their deficits? Have they done so by cutting program spending and thus reducing government's role in the economy? Or have they done so by increasing taxes, thus increasing government's role in the economy? We provide insights into all of these questions in this chapter.

If the composition of budget changes have differed over time and across jurisdictions, this raises the question as to whether certain approaches have proven more successful than others. Have expenditure-led fiscal retrenchments been more or less successful than revenue-led retrenchments? We give this issue close examination in this chapter. We then turn to a more detailed examination of the fiscal policy choices of three governments: the federal government and the provincial governments of Alberta and Ontario. This examination confirms that our estimates of the budgetary effects of fiscal policy choices accord with well-known events in the economic histories of these governments.

4.1 Identifying Discretionary Fiscal Policy

In this section, we describe the method we use to derive estimates of discretionary tax and expenditure changes.[2] We then apply the method to budget data of Canadian governments.

Efforts to identify the discretionary component of government budgets all involve some method for removing the influence on government spending and revenues of changes in *inflation, interest rates,* and *output*. The influence of inflation can most easily be removed by focussing on government spending and revenue as a fraction of GDP. While this does not afford an exact adjustment for inflation, it provides a reasonable approximation for our purposes.[3] To remove the influence of changes in interest rates on the budget, we focus on the primary deficit (the deficit net of debt servicing costs). The idea here is that movements in interest rates are due to monetary policy – both domestic and foreign – and are thus beyond the control of fiscal authorities. Changes in debt servicing costs are therefore assumed not to reflect changes in fiscal policy choices.[4]

There are a number of ways to remove the influence of cyclical movements in output from budget data. Many of these require a measure of the "potential" output of the economy – that level of output generated when all of the economy's resources are fully employed. Using this approach, one measures how revenue and expenditures would have changed had output grown at the rate of growth of potential output. Subtracting this from actual changes in revenue and expenditures identifies the change in the budget balance that was the result of a cyclical movement in output. A problem with this approach is the difficulty of determining measures of potential real output, a problem that is especially acute at the sub-national level.[5]

To avoid having to draw on measures of potential output, Blanchard's methodology uses a relatively simple measure of economic conditions – the unemployment rate – to derive estimates of discretionary fiscal policy. In particular, the approach involves estimating what government program spending and tax revenue (as a fraction of GDP) would have been this year had the unemployment rate been the same as it was last year. If this value differs from observed spending and revenue last year, it must be for the most part because of a change in fiscal policy choices. This is so because we have held economic conditions – as measured by the unemployment rate – constant when comparing these values.

This method can be applied to program expenditures and tax revenues separately. Thus, we can identify the "revenue impulse" (RI) as:

$$RI(t) = R(t)^* - R(t-1)$$

where $R(t)^*$ measures the level of tax revenue (as a fraction of GDP) in year t that would have occurred had the unemployment rate remained at the level it was in year t-1, and $R(t-1)$ measures actual, or observed, tax revenue in year t-1. If there was no change to tax rates over the year, then $R(t)^* = R(t-1)$ and the revenue impulse is zero. If tax rates have increased in year t relative to what they were in year t-1, then $R(t)^* > R(t-1)$ and the revenue impulse is positive. The size of the impulse measures the gain in revenue due solely to the discretionary policy choice to increase tax rates.

Similarly, we define the "expenditure impulse" (EI) as;

$$EI(t) = E(t)^* - E(t-1)$$

where $E(t)^*$ measures the level of program spending (as a fraction of GDP) in year t that would have occurred had the unemployment rate remained at the level it was in year t-1, and $E(t-1)$ measures observed program spending in year t-1. If there were no changes to spending propensities over the year, then $E(t)^* = E(t-1)$ and the expenditure impulse is zero. If in year t the governments spending rate increased, then $E(t)^* > E(t-1)$ and the expenditure impulse is positive. The size of the impulse measures the increase in program spending due solely to the increase in spending propensities.

Finally, we can identify a "fiscal impulse" (FI) showing the net effects of the expenditure and revenue impulses on the budget balance;

$$FI(t) = EI(t) - RI(t).$$

A positive value for the fiscal impulse indicates a combination of discretionary tax and expenditure policies that has increased the size of an existing deficit (or reduced the size of an existing surplus) while a negative value implies a combination of changes that has the effect of reducing an existing deficit (or increasing an existing surplus). A zero value for the fiscal impulse indicates either zero values for the expenditure and revenue impulses or a combination of spending and tax changes that have had an offsetting influence on the existing deficit or surplus.

The fact that the expenditure and revenue impulses can be partly or wholly off-setting in their effects in the fiscal impulse stresses the importance of decomposing fiscal impulses into the separate revenue and expenditure components. In particular, large positive expenditure impulses offset by large positive revenue impulses indicate that a government is taking an increasingly larger role in the economy even though the fiscal impulse is zero.

The data used in our analysis is inclusive of all tax revenue and all program spending, including intergovernmental grants. As discussed in Chapter 2, grants from the federal government are a key source of revenue for the provinces. However, the importance of these grants varies considerably across the provinces. For example, in fiscal year 1994/95, federal cash transfers made up an average of 43% of total provincial revenues in the Atlantic provinces, 21% in Quebec, 36% in Manitoba and 27.6% in Saskatchewan. In the "have" provinces (Ontario, Alberta and British Columbia), federal cash transfers averaged only 16% of total provincial revenues. Of these cash transfers, equalization grants were particularly important. For the Atlantic provinces, equalization payments made up an average of 59% of total cash transfers or 25% of total provincial revenues. In Quebec, equalization made up 50% of total cash transfers or 10% of total revenues. In Manitoba equalization made up 49% of cash transfers (18% of total revenues), while in Saskatchewan equalization made up 41% of cash transfers (11% of total revenues).[6]

The structure of the four major federal-provincial transfer programs – Established Program Financing (EPF), the Canada Assistance Plan (CAP), the Canada Health and Social Transfer (CHST), and the equalization program – can complicate our effort to identify discretionary budget changes over our sample period of 1961-96.[7] Several characteristics of intergovernmental grants are important for our effort to distinguish discretionary from non-discretionary policy changes. For example, the equalization program tends to remove the sensitivity of provincial revenues in many "have-not" provinces to changes in the provincial unemployment rate, since their transfers are derived solely from a five province standard of British Columbia, Alberta, Saskatchewan, Manitoba, and Ontario. As a consequence, changes in provincial revenues will appear to be insensitive to changes in provincial unemployment rates. Applying the Blanchard method to provincial revenues inclusive of equalization payments will thus cause all changes in revenue to appear to be due to discretionary choices. Or, to take another example, the revenue stabilizing feature of EPF and CAP were limited due both to their design and to various limits placed on their rates of growth. For the most part, changes in the size of EPF and CAP grants received by the provinces were relatively insensitive to changes in provincial economic conditions. Changes in the size of the CAP grant received resulting from enhancing the generosity of welfare programs, however, were clearly the result of discretionary choices made by provincial governments since the federal government was committed to meeting provincial expenditures (except after 1990 to British Columbia, Alberta, and Ontario) dollar for dollar.

For these reasons, we include EPF and CAP transfers in the definition of provincial revenues but exclude equalization grants. We recognize that to the extent that changes to the design of the EPF and CAP programs were discretionary policy changes by the federal government alone, our decision to leave these grants as part of provincial revenue means we will inaccurately "credit" this discretionary policy change to the affected provinces. This error is minimized, however, if in fact changes in the design of grant programs were negotiated by the federal and provincial governments so they share "credit" for this policy change. Similarly, we recognize that periodic changes to the design of the equalization program reflected discretionary changes involving provincial decision-makers so that we are erring in "crediting" all such changes solely to the federal government. Using this approach, we therefore measure the sensitivity of provincial revenues to changes in economic conditions prior to the revenue-equalizing effects of equalization grants but after receipt of CAP and EPF grants.[8]

The appendix to this chapter provides details on the method we use to estimate the values of $R(t)^*$ and $E(t)^*$ needed to generate values of the expenditure, revenue and fiscal impulses. The appendix also provides details on the data used to derive these estimates. These data are measured on a calendar year basis and cover the years 1961-96, inclusive, for all ten provinces and the federal government. Thus, we are able to measure revenue, expenditure, and fiscal impulses for each of 35 years (1962-1996) for 11 fiscal authorities; a total of 385 observations on each of FI, EI and RI.

Table 4-1 presents summary statistics on the fiscal, revenue and expenditure impulse by fiscal authority. Over the thirty-five years we study, the average discretionary changes to expenditures, revenues and the primary deficit (all as a fraction of GDP) have generally not differed significantly from zero. This is not that surprising given the length of the period and the variety of economic conditions and policy-makers determining the fiscal policy choices used to calculate these averages. It is worth noting that Newfoundland and PEI stand out as having introduced impulses with larger standard deviations than other jurisdictions. In part, this reflects the fact that the provincial government's share of provincial GDP is quite large in these provinces; provincial government spending and taxation is twice the share of provincial GDP in Newfoundland and PEI as it is in Ontario. As a consequence, the same per capita government expenditure will show up as a larger fiscal impulse in Newfoundland than in Ontario. We will return to this issue in the next section.

Table 4-1: Summary Statistics on Fiscal, Revenue, and Expenditure Impulses, 1962-96

	Nfld	PEI	NS	NB	Quebec	Ontario	Manitoba	Sask.	Alberta	BC	All Provinces	Federal	Federal + Provinces
Fiscal Impulse													
μ	-0.15	-0.08	-0.07	-0.12	-0.12	-0.08	-0.12	-0.24	-0.09	-0.03	-0.11	-0.13	-0.11
ø	3.34	2.84	1.47	1.68	0.88	0.50	0.96	1.71	1.78	0.83	1.79	0.89	1.73
Expenditure Impulse													
μ	0.27	0.14	0.28	0.29	0.35	0.20	0.26	0.15	0.06	0.30	0.23	-0.05	0.21
ø	2.54	2.70	1.32	2.53	1.01	0.62	0.97	1.53	1.58	0.94	1.71	0.68	1.65
Revenue Impulse													
μ	0.42	0.22	0.35	0.41	0.47	0.28	0.38	0.38	0.16	0.33	0.34	0.08	0.32
ø	3.01	2.53	1.26	1.64	0.73	0.43	0.84	1.35	1.09	0.64	1.55	0.71	1.49

μ= mean value, ø = standard deviation of the sample.

Before discussing these impulses further, we offer an evaluation of our adopted methodology by comparing the fiscal impulses derived using this method to those obtained using an alternative approach. Figure 4-1 presents two measures of the discretionary fiscal impulse contained within the federal government's budget for the 1963-95 period. The bars identified as "Unemployment Adjusted" present discretionary fiscal impulses derived in the way described above. Those identified as "GDP Adjusted" present the impulses calculated by the federal government's Department of Finance. The method employed by the Department of Finance involves calculating potential real GDP and using this measure to cyclically adjust the federal primary deficit. The fiscal impulse so derived measures the change in the cyclically adjusted primary deficit as a percentage of potential GDP. The method employed by the Department of Finance, then, uses a measure of potential GDP, rather than last period's unemployment rate, as a benchmark for removing the cyclical influence from budget data. Unfortunately, such an estimate is available only for the federal budget and for all eleven fiscal authorities in aggregate. This is due to the difficulty in obtaining reliable estimates of potential real GDP for individual provinces. As such, it would be reassuring if the method we employ to derive fiscal impulses – a method that can be as readily applied to provincial as federal budget data – generates results similar to those generated by the alternative method employed by the Department of Finance.

Figure 4-1: Alternative Measures of the Federal Governments Fiscal Impulse

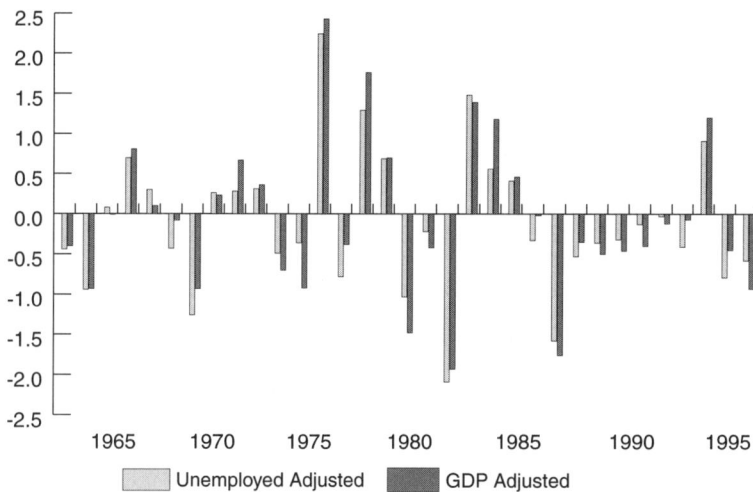

Figure 4-1 shows that the two methods do indeed produce very similar estimates of the discretionary fiscal impulse contained within the federal primary deficit. Only one observation fails to move in the same direction (1965) and the difference is quite small. Moreover, although the estimates generated by the Department of Finance more often than not assign a slightly larger share of the total change in the deficit to discretionary policy, the two methods identify similar magnitudes. It is thus with some confidence that we employ the methodology we have adopted. Another way of increasing our confidence in the methodology is to see if it identifies well-known discretionary policy changes. This is something to which we return below.

4.2 The Characteristics of Past Fiscal Policies

A government's overall fiscal stance is determined by the size of the fiscal impulses generated by discretionary policy changes. In particular, we define a stance to be "neutral" if the fiscal impulse is small (plus or minus 0.5% of GDP). Similarly, a stance is "loose" if the fiscal impulse increases the existing primary deficit by a moderate amount (between 0.5% and 1.5% of GDP), and the fiscal stance is "very loose" if the fiscal impulse leads to a substantial increase in the primary deficit (in excess of 1.5% of GDP). "Tight" and "very tight" stances are those that move the deficit equal magnitudes in the opposite direction. The following schematic represents our characterization of loose and tight discretionary fiscal policy.

Very Tight Stance	Tight Stance	Neutral Stance	Loose Stance	Very Loose Stance

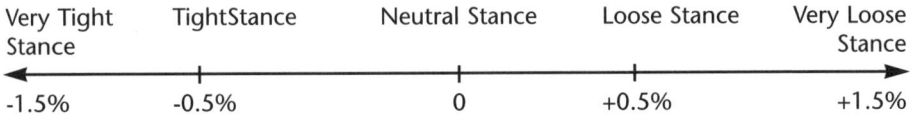

-1.5%	-0.5%	0	+0.5%	+1.5%

In choosing these cut-off points we tried to achieve a reasonable trade-off between the requirement that very loose and very tight stances be significantly different from a neutral stance, and the requirement that we obtain a reasonable number of observations on each category of fiscal stance. Table 4-2 provides summary statistics on each type of fiscal stance for each fiscal authority. These summary statistics indicate that the cut-off points for defining fiscal stances do indeed provide us with a reason-

Table 4-2: Summary Statistics on Fiscal Stances, 1962-96

	Nfld	PEI	NS	NB	Quebec	Ontario	Manitoba	Sask.	Alberta	BC	All Provinces	Federal	Federal + Provinces
Neutral													
n	7	5	7	9	15	23	18	12	6	18	120	17	137
μ	-0.11	-0.14	-0.01	-0.19	-0.01	-0.02	0.02	0.00	-0.01	0.12	-0.01	-0.11	-0.02
ø	0.28	0.31	0.32	0.27	0.30	0.25	0.25	0.27	0.25	0.21	0.27	0.32	0.27
Loose													
n	4	7	7	4	8	4	4	8	6	6	58	7	65
μ	1.02	0.95	0.96	0.80	0.83	0.86	0.93	1.11	1.07	0.98	0.96	0.89	0.95
ø	0.50	0.34	0.28	0.23	0.30	0.24	0.23	0.23	0.33	0.30	0.29	0.36	0.30
Tight													
n	6	5	8	9	7	8	9	3	8	8	71	8	79
μ	-0.81	-1.11	-0.96	-0.89	-0.78	-0.72	-0.95	-0.98	-0.85	-0.93	-0.89	-0.91	-0.89
ø	0.36	0.30	0.32	0.23	0.25	0.13	0.24	0.46	0.33	0.24	0.28	0.30	0.28
Very Loose													
n	7	9	6	6	1	0	2	3	6	1	41	1	42
μ	4.37	3.11	2.11	2.85	1.69	- -	2.18	2.60	2.73	1.77	2.94	2.24	2.92
ø	3.44	2.35	0.46	0.84	- -	- -	0.75	1.33	1.02	- -	1.95	- -	1.93
Very Tight													
n	11	9	7	7	4	0	2	9	9	2	60	2	62
μ	-3.12	-3.45	-2.03	-2.09	-1.73	- -	-2.03	-2.44	-2.15	-1.74	-2.50	-1.83	-2.48
ø	2.42	1.67	0.52	0.57	0.22	- -	0.62	1.08	0.50	0.20	1.41	0.36	1.39

n = number of observations, μ = mean value, ø = standard deviation of the sample.
- - = too few observations to calculate.

able number of observations for each category of fiscal stance. The cut-offs also seem reasonable in light of the fact that for the full sample of 385 observations the standard deviation is 1.73 and the mean value of a neutral stance is -0.11; thus very tight and very loose fiscal stances are roughly one standard deviation or better from a neutral stance.

It is interesting to note that the values in the last column of Table 4-2 are very similar to those reported by Alesina and Perotti in their study of 20 OECD countries using a similar approach.[9] For the OECD data, they find that on average very loose and very tight stances are associated with fiscal impulses equal to 2.81% and -2.61% of GDP, respectively, versus our estimates of 2.92% and -2.48%. Similarly, their estimates of 0.93% and -0.93% of GDP for loose and tight stances are very similar to our estimates of 0.95% and -0.89%. Given that 350 of our 385 observations come from provincial budget data, this says something about the freedom of Canadian provinces to use budget deficits and surpluses to finance budget changes; their freedom to do so is on par with OECD countries. It also makes Canadian provinces a useful additional observation on the sort of government behaviour Alesina and Perotti seek to describe using OECD data. Any differences in results do not seem likely to be due to differences in the constraints under which provinces and OECD countries operate.

Finally, just as Alesina and Perotti discovered for OECD countries, we find that very loose fiscal stances are virtually mirror images of very tight fiscal stances; the average increase in the cyclically adjusted primary deficit under a very loose stance is very close, in absolute value, to the average decrease in the cyclically adjusted primary deficit under a very tight stance. The same pattern is true of loose versus tight stances. This pattern is generally true for each individual fiscal authority as well. An implication of this is that quantitative differences in the characteristics of (very) loose and (very) tight stances will be due to qualitative differences in fiscal choices and not due to differences in the size of one stance versus another.

Earlier, we raised an issue that might cause one to object to this definition of fiscal stances. That is, if government's share of provincial GDP differs substantially across provinces, then a given percentage change in the government deficit will generate a larger change as a fraction of GDP (that is, a larger fiscal impulse) in a province where the government's share is large than it will in a province where the government's share is relatively small. As we noted, this is in fact an issue for Canadian provinces. One way of dealing with this problem is to define a fiscal stance relative to the size of the mean and standard deviation of fiscal impulses in each province. Thus, for example, a fiscal impulse in PEI would be categorized as very loose only if its value exceeded one standard deviation from the average; an amount observed to be equal to 2.66% of

GDP from Table 3-2. Similarly, to be classified as very tight, a fiscal impulse in PEI would need to exceed -3.07% of GDP. We have found that our results are not terribly sensitive to switching to this definition.[10] As a consequence, we adopt the definition we have because it makes for easier interpretation of many of the results that follow.

Table 4-3   The Characteristics of Fiscal Stances

Fiscal Stance	Number of Observations	Average Fiscal Impulse	Average Expenditure Impulse	Average Revenue Impulse
All	385	-0.11 (0.09)	0.21 (0.08)	0.32 (0.08)
Neutral	137	- 0.02 (0.02)	0.28 (0.06)	0.31 (0.05)
Loose	65	0.95 (0.04)	0.70 (0.07)	-0.25 (0.06)
Tight	79	-0.89 (0.03)	-0.33 (0.07)	0.56 (0.07)
Very Loose	42	2.92 (0.30)	2.30 (0.16)	-0.62 (0.12)
Very Tight	62	-2.48 (0.18)	-1.22 (0.09)	1.25 (0.11)

The values in parentheses are standard deviations of the mean.

Discretionary changes in deficits can be achieved by introducing (i) discretionary changes to expenditures, (ii) discretionary changes to taxes, or (iii) some combination of these. Our goal in this section is to characterize fiscal stances by identifying the extent to which each is composed of changes to spending as opposed to tax revenue. Changes in discretionary spending and tax revenue are identified in the same way as we identify discretionary changes in the budget, via the use of EI and RI.

Table 4-3 decomposes the average fiscal impulses into the expenditure and revenue components. This allows us to investigate whether various stances have tended to be dominated by discretionary changes to revenues or expenditures.

Table 4-3 illustrates an interesting symmetry between very tight and very loose fiscal stances. When Canadian governments have introduced discretionary budget changes intended to *increase* the deficit by over

1.5% of GDP (a very loose stance), they have, on average, done so by increasing program expenditures by 2.30% of GDP while introducing a much smaller reduction in taxes of 0.62% of GDP. To put this into perspective, if the federal government had adopted a very loose discretionary stance in 1996, by the standards of the past these averages suggest that it would be characterized by an increase in spending of almost $19 billion and a decrease in revenues of about $5 billion, for a combined $24 billion dollar increase in the deficit.

When, however, Canadian governments have introduced discretionary budget changes intended to *decrease* the deficit by over 1.5% of GDP (a very tight stance), they have, on average, done so with a "balanced" approach of increasing taxes (by 1.25% of GDP) by virtually the same amount by which they decreased program expenditures (by 1.22% of GDP) – amounts equal to about $10 billion at the federal level in 1996. A roughly similar pattern exists for loose versus tight fiscal stances, though the sense of "balance" observed in very tight stances is less prevalent in tight stances. Loose stances are dominated by increases in program spending while tight stances are dominated by increases in tax revenue. It is also interesting to note that over all stances, although offsetting in their net impact on the primary deficit, the average annual change in expenditures and tax revenue are separately economically significant at 0.21% and 0.32% of GDP respectively.

These results are worthy of note because they suggest a systematic bias in the historical fiscal policy of Canadian governments. The tendency to use expenditure-dominant loose fiscal policy and a more balanced approach to tight fiscal policy leads inevitably to a growing share of GDP absorbed by government budgets – and indeed we have observed this over the 1962-96 period studied. It suggests a bias to adopting fiscal policy that increases (or at least does not decrease) the role of government in the economy; a result that most will not find all that surprising. Nevertheless, it is important to keep this result in mind when we discuss the nature of more recent fiscal policy choices later in section 4.4

Table 4-4:	Types of Very Tight and Very Loose Stances		
	Expenditure-Dominant	Tax-Dominant	Neither Expenditure-nor Tax-Dominant
Very Tight Stances	24	20	18
Very Loose Stances	25	9	8

Averages such as these can be misleading, however, since a small number of observations of extremely large changes may bias the average in one direction or the other. In Table 4-4, we report the *number* of very tight and very loose fiscal stances that were dominated by spending changes or by tax changes. In particular, we define a stance to be "expenditure-dominant" if the expenditure impulse makes up 70% or more of the total fiscal impulse. Similarly, a "tax-dominant" stance is defined as one where the revenue impulse makes up 70% or more of the total fiscal impulse.

The low number of tax-dominant very loose stances over the 1962-1996 period is striking. Discretionary policy intended to increase the primary deficit mainly via a tax cut was observed just 9 times. The 20 observations of tax-dominant very tight stances indicates tax changes were more prevalent when the choice was to reduce the deficit (and thereby increase taxes) than when it is to increase the deficit (and thereby cut

---

Table 4-5: Changing Government's Share of GDP Via Very Tight and Very Loose Stances

a. Reducing Government's Share of GDP

Expenditure-Dominant Very Tight Stances:

Newfoundland	1968, 1969, 1984, 1995
Prince Edward Is.	1968, 1978
Nova Scotia	1983
New Brunswick	1978, 1979, 1983, 1993, 1995
Quebec	1978, 1987
Manitoba	1984
Saskatchewan	1962, 1993, 1994
Alberta	1968, 1973, 1980, 1984, 1993
British Columbia	1984

Tax-Dominant Very Loose Stances:

Newfoundland	1963, 1988
Prince Edward Is.	1973, 1983, 1996
Nova Scotia	1981
Manitoba	1973
Saskatchewan	1986, 1991

b. Increasing Government's Share of GDP

Expenditure-Dominant Very Loose Stances:

Newfoundland	1964, 1967, 1971, 1982
Prince Edward Is.	1963, 1966, 1974, 1977, 1992
Nova Scotia	1966, 1970, 1992
New Brunswick	1964, 1967, 1975, 1980, 1982
Quebec	1975
Manitoba	1992
Saskatchewan	1970
Alberta	1966, 1979, 1986, 1992
British Columbia	1991

Tax-Dominant Very Tight Stances:

Newfoundland	1965, 1970, 1985, 1987 1992, 1996
Prince Edward Is.	1969, 1975, 1984
Nova Scotia	1977, 1980, 1996
Quebec	1995
Saskatchewan	1971, 1974, 1983, 1989
Alberta	1974, 1988
Federal	1981

taxes). Put another way, a preference for spending over tax changes is more prevalent when the choice is to increase the deficit than when the choice is to decrease the deficit. The "balanced" approach to deficit change found greater favour when large deficit reductions were enacted than when large deficit increases were introduced.

Table 4-5 identifies the governments that initiated expenditure-dominant and tax-dominant very tight and very loose stances and the years in which they did so. Panel (a) identifies expenditure- and tax-dominant budget changes that reflected a decision by the government to reduce its share of GDP. Panel (b) identifies expenditure and tax-dominant budget changes that reflected a decision by the government to increase its share of GDP.

New Brunswick and Alberta tie for introducing the greatest number of expenditure-dominant stances designed to reduce government's share of the economy. Prince Edward Island introduced the greatest number of tax-dominant stances designed to reduce government's share of the economy. As the table shows, seven of the 33 expenditure- or tax-dominant stances designed to reduce government's share of the economy were introduced after 1992. Thus, the frequency of such stances has increased substantially. Interestingly, New Brunswick also ties (with Prince Edward Island) for introducing the greatest number of expenditure-dominant stances designed to increase government's share of the economy.

Also of note are the observations not included in Table 4-5. In particular, the period following the 1993 federal budget, often perceived as heralding a period of large and significant attacks on the deficit, shows up in our calculations as yielding only moderately tight discretionary stances in 1994, 1995 and 1996; stances averaging 0.9% of GDP in each year. Although these stances did not meet the standard required to be classified as very tight, they were, however, expenditure-dominant. Also absent from Table 4-5 is any sign of a series of tax-dominant very tight stances from Saskatchewan in the 1990s. A popular perception is that the dramatic improvement in Saskatchewan's deficit during the 1990s was due to large tax increases. Here we see evidence instead of very tight stances, in 1993 and 1994, driven by expenditure cuts. Similarly, the budget cuts in Ontario by the Harris government did not prove so large as to be classified as very tight. From 1993-96 inclusive, the Ontario government introduced four straight tight stances averaging 0.74% of GDP per year. On average, these stances also proved to be expenditure-dominant. Finally, while the first two years of the budget cuts introduced by the Klein government in Alberta meet the requirement to be labelled very tight, only the first year, 1993, was expenditure-dominant. Thus, the perception that the improvement in Alberta's finances is solely due to expenditure cuts needs closer examination. We will discuss government-specific stances in more detail in section 4.5.

Table 4.6: Concerted Efforts at Deficit Reduction and Expansion, 1962-96

Newfoundland:	1968-70	VT, VT, VT		**Ontario:**	1990-92	L, L, L
	1976-78	T, VT, T			1993-96	T, T, T, T
Prince Ed. Is.	1972-74	L, VL, VL		**Alberta:**	1981-83	L, VL, VL
					1993-95	VT, VT, T
Nova Scotia:	1982-85	T, VT, T, T		**Federal:**	1994-96	T, T, T
	1994-96	VT, T, VT				
New Brunswick:	1983-86	VT, VT, T, T				

VT denotes very tight, VL denotes very loose, L denotes loose and T denotes tight stances.

Another revealing way of characterizing particular fiscal stances is according to whether or not they were part of a strong commitment to deficit reduction or expansion over a number of years. Table 4-6 identifies concerted efforts to expand or contract deficits; concerted in the sense that three straight non-neutral discretionary fiscal impulses in the same direction were introduced. There is a possibility that more examples of such concerted efforts might be added as data for years after 1996 become available. For example, in 1995 and 1996, Newfoundland introduced two very tight stances, New Brunswick introduced a very tight and a tight stance, and Quebec introduced two very tight stances.

It is interesting to note the prevalence of concerted efforts by the Atlantic provinces to reduce the size of their deficits. It has been suggested elsewhere that these efforts were likely prompted by the heavy debt load of these provinces and by the further incentive wrought by decreases in debt ratings.[11] We presented some evidence in support of this view in the previous chapter dealing with sustainability. From this perspective, it is also interesting to note the absence of concerted efforts on the part of the federal government prior to the tight stance in 1994. The lack of concerted efforts by the federal government is rather disturbing since it had the most rapidly growing debt/GDP ratio of the eleven Canadian fiscal authorities over the 1975-96 period. This is a subject we expand on in Chapter 6.

Table 4-7 presents measures of the characteristics of fiscal stances by decade. Our objective here is to get some idea of the extent to which the composition of each type of stance has changed over time. Looking first at the characteristics of the average stance, we observe that the average fiscal impulse, which was quite small in the first three decades, has in the 1990s taken on a substantially larger negative value. Canadian gov-

Table 4-7: The Characteristics of Fiscal Stances, Decade Averages

	1962-69	1970-79	1980-89	1990-96
All Stances				
Number	88	110	110	77
Average FI	-0.09	0.02	-0.09	-0.35
Average EI	0.54	0.36	0.04	-0.15
Average RI	0.63	0.34	0.13	0.20
Loose Stances				
Number	12	19	22	12
Average FI	0.94	0.94	1.04	0.81
Average EI	0.79	0.62	0.69	0.77
Average RI	-0.15	-0.32	-0.35	-0.04
Very Loose Stances				
Number	9	13	12	8
Average FI	3.67	2.53	3.49	1.87
Average EI	3.92	2.16	1.97	1.19
Average RI	0.26	-0.37	-1.52	-0.68
Tight Stances				
Number	19	19	22	19
Average FI	-0.83	-0.93	-0.86	-0.95
Average EI	0.17	-0.49	-0.39	-0.59
Average RI	1.00	0.44	0.46	0.36
Very Tight Stances				
Number	11	15	20	16
Average FI	-3.26	-1.97	-2.78	-2.04
Average EI	-1.95	-0.68	-1.13	-1.36
Average RI	1.32	1.29	1.65	0.69

ernments in the 1990s have introduced discretionary policies that reduced their deficit to GDP ratios by an average of 0.35 percentage points of GDP per year. This change in direction is due to decisions to introduce expenditure *cuts* averaging 0.15 percentage points of GDP whereas in previous decades, the 1960s especially, the average stance introduced spending *increases*. The move toward spending cuts has more than offset the effect on the deficit of a move toward introducing substantially smaller revenue impulses.

The characteristics of loose stances have remained more or less constant over time. Tight stances, on the other hand, have changed considerably sine the 1960s. Relative to the 1960s, negative tight fiscal impulses have occurred more because of expenditure cuts and less because of revenue increases. The fiscal impulses associated with very loose stances are much smaller in the 1990s than previously. This is due to the fact that the increase in program expenditures characteristic of very loose stances have become steadily smaller and because revenue changes, which were positive in the 1960s, became negative thereafter. Very tight stances have also grown smaller (in absolute value) over time. This is due to a reduction in the size of the revenue increases and a reduction (of equal magnitude) in the size of the expenditure cuts associated with very tight stances.

The data in Table 4-7 also suggest that very tight and very loose stances have each become smaller in absolute value. What's more, very tight stances, which over the entire 1962-96 period exhibit a balance between expenditure cuts and revenue increases, in the 1990s have become more unbalanced in favour of spending cuts. Similarly, very loose stances, which over the entire 1962-96 period exhibit a strong bias toward spending increases, in the 1980s and 1990s are more evenly balanced between spending increases and revenue reductions. Thus, governments have reduced their reliance on increasing revenues as a fraction of GDP and have turned toward cuts to expenditures. In our view this represents an important turnaround in the approach to fiscal policy in Canada.

4.3 Successful Retrenchments?

The fact that there have been such a variety of approaches to deficit reduction, both across governments and over time, raises the question as to whether certain approaches might be more "successful" than others.

In their examination of the fiscal impulses of OECD countries, Alesina and Perotti identified "successful" and "unsuccessful" fiscal retrenchments by looking for very tight fiscal stances that were followed, in the next three years, by primary deficits (as a fraction of GDP) that were, on average, below the initial deficit by 1.5% of GDP.[12] As such, they consider a fiscal retrenchment to be a success if it has "staying power", and results in a long lasting decline in the deficit/GDP ratio. They then analyze the characteristics of "successful" retrenchments to determine whether they are dominated by expenditure decreases, tax increases, or some combination of both. They find that successful fiscal retrenchments in OECD countries tend to be characterized by expenditure cuts, rather than tax increases. This result was emphasized by the government of Ontario in its 1996 budget documents as evidence that expenditure-led fiscal retrenchments are especially successful at permanently reducing deficits.[13] Of course, it (almost) goes without saying that this approach to evaluating the "success" of fiscal policy is very narrow and should not be interpreted as having any normative significance.

In considering what is required for a "successful" fiscal retrenchment under the "staying power" standard, it is important to recognize that a government may choose to adopt a very tight stance for reasons other than permanently reducing future deficits. A government may reduce the deficit in the current period as part of a long-term plan to permanently reduce the size of deficits, or it may introduce such a stance as a temporary measure that is part of an effort at discretionary stabilization policy. One might expect that the composition of a very tight stance – that is, the set of tax and expenditure changes defining the stance – would look very different depending on whether its purpose was to act as a stabilization policy or as a deficit reduction program.

Alesina and Perotti do not identify very tight stances intended as part of a discretionary stabilization effort, nor do they distinguish these from stances intended to permanently reduce current and future deficits. Their implicit assumption is that all fiscal retrenchments represent initial efforts to permanently reduce deficits. If this is not true, then the failure of very tight stances to cause permanent deficit reductions might not be surprising. Indeed, given the likelihood that OECD countries used fiscal policy as a short-run stabilization policy tool – something that was especially likely during the 1960s and early 1970s when Keynesianism was in its heyday and debt/GDP ratios were not worrisomely high – it might be considered surprising that Alesina and Perotti obtained such strong evidence of current fiscal retrenchments being correlated with smaller deficits in the future.

It is also important to note that changes in budget policy may also be due to the fact that a new government, with a new fiscal philosophy or agenda, has been elected. Thus, a very tight stance in the current period may prove unsuccessful by Alesina and Perotti's definition only because the government which implemented the stance was superseded by a new government. In labelling such a stance as "unsuccessful", Alesina and

Table 4-8: "Successful" versus "Unsuccessful" Very Tight Fiscal Retrenchments

	Successful	Unsuccessful
Number	28	22
Average Expenditure Impulse	-1.51	-0.87
Average Revenue Impulse	0.90	1.90
Average Fiscal Impulse	-2.41	-2.77

Note: *The sum of successful and unsuccessful stances is less than the number of very tight stances reported in previous tables because the need to evaluate a stance by looking ahead 3 periods. Thus some observations were lost.*

Perotti seem to have in mind the idea that if a very tight stance was followed by loose or very loose stances, this is an indication that the very tight stance failed to cut the deficit in such a way to prevent subsequent discretionary increases in the deficit from creeping back. Thus, the stance was unsuccessful for failing to control the future behaviour of legislators. From this perspective, a very tight stance is successful only if it prevents future stances that are (very) loose. But assuming this change in direction reflects the wishes of voters, Alesina and Perotti's definition means success is possible only if the very tight stance can be imposed in such a way as to circumvent the wishes of future voters.

With these caveats in mind, we nonetheless apply the Alesina and Perotti definition of successful fiscal retrenchments to the sixty-two cases of very tight fiscal stances we previously identified in our data on Canadian federal and provincial budgets. Table 4-8 reports our findings.

The results are quite similar to what Alesina and Perotti found for OECD data. In particular, "successful" retrenchments, in the sense of high "staying power", have been much more heavily weighted toward expenditure cuts than revenue increases, while the average unsuccessful retrenchment was more oriented toward tax increases than spending cuts. What's more, we find no evidence that the size of the fiscal retrenchment has anything to do with it being successful; we find that both successful and unsuccessful retrenchments tend to be of similar magnitude. This is quite important, as it seems to go against the commonly expressed wisdom that fiscal retrenchments have to be large in order to "stick".

Before drawing any conclusions from these results, it is important to note that of the twenty-eight successful retrenchments making up this average, fifteen were expenditure-dominant, six were tax-dominant, and seven were neither tax- nor expenditure-dominant. Thus, the average discretionary changes in expenditures and taxes reported in Table 4-8 hide a good deal of variation. What's more, of the twenty-eight successful retrenchments, fifteen were followed by one or more very tight stances within the three year window used for evaluating whether the stance was successful. Another three cases were followed by two or more tight stances within the three year window. Similarly, of the twenty-two unsuccessful retrenchments, seventeen were followed by one or more very loose stances and one was followed by two or more loose stances within the three year window. Clearly, there is good reason for many of the successful retrenchments to have proved "successful" and there is good reason why eighteen of the twenty-two "unsuccessful" retrenchments failed to pass the criteria for success.

But there is a more fundamental question here. What we are ultimately interested in, when we ask whether certain retrenching budgets have a more prolonged influence on future deficits than others, is whether governments partake in so-called "tax and spend" behaviour or "spend and tax" behaviour. "Tax and spend" behaviour suggests that should a government make a choice to increase taxes in a particular year, this simply encourages future governments to increase spending in future years. Thus, it is argued, cutting deficits via tax increases is futile in the long run – it just leads to more spending. Similarly, "spend and tax" behaviour suggests that having made the choice to increase spending in a year commits the government to financing this expenditure in the future as a constituency quickly builds to defend the spending program. Thus, taxes must rise in the future to finance these expenditures. To examine these issues requires an examination of the direction of causality between changes in discretionary program spending and discretionary changes in revenue.

Table 4-9 presents the results of simple *Granger causality tests* between the revenue and the expenditure impulse. Granger causality tests are an attempt to determine the direction of causation between two variables, which is exactly what we want to get at – do taxes cause spending, or does spending cause taxes? We find strong evidence that federal revenue impulses have tended to *Granger-cause* federal expenditure impulses, whereas the opposite is not true. In other words, we find evidence of "tax and spend" behaviour on the part of the federal government – discretionary revenue changes cause discretionary spending changes. This suggests that, for the federal government, deficit reduction efforts dominated by tax increases have historically tended to be futile, as these tax increases have attracted higher spending down the road.

With regard to the provinces, we find evidence to support the hypothesis of "spend and tax" behaviour in Nova Scotia; discretionary spending changes cause discretionary revenue changes. There is weaker evidence of this also being true in British Columbia. For the most part, however, discretionary spending changes at the provincial level are independent of discretionary revenue changes – the Granger-causality tests are unable to uncover causation running in either direction.

What do we conclude about the impact of current fiscal stances on future deficits? We think we have provided some "made in Canada" support for the following two conclusions. First, we think that the methodology used by Alesina and Perotti to identify "successful" fiscal retrenchments can give misleading results – at least for Canadian governments. Thus, while it is true that applying their methodology to Canadian data yields results similar to what they found for OECD countries, we have some concerns about the interpretation of these results. Second, we think that causality tests are a better way of investigating the question of whether expenditure or tax-led

Table 4-9: Granger Causality Tests

Jurisdiction	Dependent Variable	Independent Variable	Number of Lags*	Significance Level
Newfoundland	EI	RI	1	0.775
	RI	EI	1	0.586
Prince Edward Is.	EI	RI	2	0.631
	RI	EI	1	0.583
Nova Scotia	EI	RI	1	0.691
	RI	EI	2	0.028
New Brunswick	EI	RI	1	0.542
	RI	EI	1	0.765
Quebec	EI	RI	1	0.825
	RI	EI	3	0.258
Ontario	EI	RI	1	0.176
	RI	EI	1	0.728
Manitoba	EI	RI	1	0.741
	RI	EI	1	0.859
Saskatchewan	EI	RI	1	0.704
	RI	EI	2	0.256
Alberta	EI	RI	1	0.861
	RI	EI	1	0.705
British Columbia	EI	RI	2	0.149
	RI	EI	3	0.086
Federal Gov't	EI	RI	3	0.005
	RI	EI	1	0.316

* Lag lengths were selected on the basis of the Akaike information criteria.
N = 32 for each jurisdiction. In prior testing, all series but Nova Scotia's RI were found to be stationary in levels.

retrenchments are more or less successful, in the sense of being less likely to be reversed in the future. Applying causality tests to our measures of expenditure and revenue impulses, we find evidence that the federal government engages in "tax and spend" behaviour. For the federal government, then, past behaviour suggests that deficit reduction efforts that rely on tax increases may be ineffective in producing a long lasting reduction in the deficit. Indeed, tax increases tend to eventually lead to spending increases and hence a growing government share of the economy. For the federal government, deficit reduction via spending cuts seems to be the preferred option in the case of fiscal retrenchments. At the provincial level, deficit reduction via spending cuts or tax increases seem capable of being equally effective (or ineffective); there is no consistent pattern of current tax or spending changes causing future spending or tax changes.

4.4 Recent Efforts at Fiscal Retrenchments

The last four years of our sample period, 1993 to 1996 inclusive, were years of economic recovery in Canada. The unemployment rate fell from 11.2% to 9.7% during these years. The recovery was rather uneven throughout the country, however. The unemployment rate fell by 3.4 percentage points in PEI, 2.4 percentage points in Alberta and 2.2 percentage points in Manitoba. At the other end of the scale, the unemployment rate fell by just 0.6 percentage points in Nova Scotia and 0.7 percentage points in Newfoundland. Such wide differences in the rate of economic recovery is what makes comparing deficit reduction efforts across provinces challenging; clearly, Nova Scotia and Newfoundland would find it much more difficult to reduce their deficit/GDP ratios than would PEI and Alberta.

In Table 4-10 we present, for each government, our calculations of the sum of "observed" fiscal impulses (OFI) and the sum of (discretionary) fiscal impulses (FI). By "observed" fiscal impulse we mean the percentage point change in the *total* deficit/GDP ratio, where the measure of the observed deficit is all inclusive; it includes the debt service component and, for the provinces, equalization grant revenue. Changes in this ratio are due to changes in economic conditions affecting automatic stabilizers, changes in interest rates affecting the debt service component, and to discretionary policy actions. As explained previously, the sum of the fiscal impulses (FI) is a measure of the extent of discretionary policy actions. The ratio of FI to OFI, reported in the last

Table 4-10: Recent Budget Policies, 1993-96

	Sum of FI	Sum of EI	Sum of RI	Sum of OFI	FI/OFI
Newfoundland	-3.48	-3.09	0.40	-2.64	1.32
Prince Edward Is.	-2.63	-6.57	-3.94	-2.16	1.22
Nova Scotia	-4.27	-2.64	1.63	-5.06	0.84
New Brunswick	-5.07	-4.28	0.79	-4.03	1.26
Quebec	-2.64	-2.04	0.60	-2.40	1.10
Ontario	-2.98	-2.53	0.46	-3.13	0.95
Manitoba	-4.14	-4.11	0.03	-5.30	0.78
Saskatchewan	-7.21	-8.73	-1.52	-8.16	0.88
Alberta	-4.26	-6.70	-2.44	-5.29	0.81
British Columbia	-1.81	-1.24	0.57	-1.93	0.94
Federal Gov't	-1.83	-2.67	-0.84	-2.63	0.70

column, indicates the fraction of the reduction in the observed deficit/GDP ratio due solely to discretionary changes in fiscal policy choices initiated by the identified government. For example, the value reported for the federal government, 0.70, indicates that of the 2.63 percentage point reduction in the observed federal deficit/GDP ratio (from 4.03% in 1992 to 1.41% in 1996), 70% of this was due to discretionary actions taken on the part of government to reduce program spending and/or increase tax revenue. The remaining 30% of this reduction was due to the effects of automatic stabilizers on revenues and expenditures and the effect of falling interest rates on debt servicing costs. Thus, by our calculations, of the approximately $20 billion reduction in the federal deficit that occurred over this period, about $14 billion of the reduction was due to discretionary government policy and $6 billion due to favourable economic conditions.

The table indicates that a large part of the fiscal retrenchment that occurred between 1993 and 1996 was indeed due to discretionary choices. It is interesting to note that while the value of the FI/OFI ratio for the federal government is large, it is nonetheless the lowest value for the eleven fiscal authorities. The government of Saskatchewan, for example, realized a much larger reduction in its observed deficit/GDP ratio (from a deficit of 4.56% in 1992 to a surplus of 3.60% in 1996), and 88% of this was due to discretionary actions taken by that government. Thus, of the over $2 billion turn around in the budget balance of Saskatchewan over this period, $1.8 billion was due to discretionary actions on the part of the government.

Ratios in excess of unity indicate that economic conditions over this period were such that they contributed to a worsening of the government's fiscal position despite the government's efforts to the contrary. Thus, Newfoundland found that despite the introduction of discretionary budget changes that would reduce its deficit/GDP ratio over this period, these efforts were offset by economic conditions that moved its deficit/GDP ratio in the opposite direction. If not for its discretionary policy changes over this period, Newfoundland's deficit/GDP ratio would have increased by 0.8 percentage points over this period.

Table 4-10 also identifies for each government the source of change in the fiscal impulse. All eleven fiscal authorities introduced discretionary policy changes that reduced their expenditure/GDP ratios. The largest of these changes was the government of Saskatchewan which introduced discretionary measures to reduce the ratio of program spending to GDP by 8.7 percentage points. Interestingly, the government of Alberta, often considered to be the champion of expenditure cuts, is second, though with a still very significant 6.7 percentage point discretionary reduction in its ratio of program spending to GDP (almost $6 billion in discretionary budget cuts). The smallest of these changes was due to the government of British Columbia which introduced policy changes to reduce the ratio of program spending to GDP by just 1.2 percentage points.

Although the cuts to federal program spending are sometimes advertised (by the federal government) as extreme, here we see that at 2.7 percentage points of GDP, the federal government over the 1993-96 period introduced cuts to program spending that were much less than the average introduced by the provinces (4.2 percentage points). Nonetheless, our calculations show that the federal government instituted over $20 billion in discretionary budget cuts over this period. It is also important to note that the cuts to federal spending include cuts to provincial grants; an amount equal to 1.0% of GDP (about $8 billion). Thus discretionary cuts to federal "own" spending over this period was a rather more modest 1.7% of GDP (about $12 billion).

A negative value in the "Sum of RI" column indicates that tax revenue as a fraction of GDP was reduced due to discretionary policy choices. In particular, it indicates the fall in the ratio of tax revenue to GDP that would have occurred had the unemployment rate stayed constant from one year to the next during the period 1993-96. A positive value indicates tax revenue as a fraction of GDP has been increased due to discretionary policy choices. Only the federal government and three provinces, PEI, Saskatchewan and Alberta, introduced policies that had the effect of reducing their revenue/GDP ratios.[14] The remaining seven provinces all introduced measures that increased their tax revenue as a fraction of GDP. Nova Scotia introduced the largest increase mainly via the introduction of a substantial income surtax, an increase in the provincial sales tax rate, a widening of the sales tax base, and an increase in the gasoline tax, all in the1993 tax year.[15]

The period 1993-96 is noteworthy because during it, most Canadian governments introduced substantial discretionary measures to reduce their deficits and did so mainly by decreasing program expenditures. As we saw earlier, this behaviour differs substantially from their behaviour in the past, when deficit reductions were more evenly balanced between measures to reduce program expenditures and increase revenues.

This may auger well for the permanency of the deficit reduction effort. In section 4.3 we provided some evidence that expenditure-lead fiscal retrenchments (deficit reductions) may prove to be longer lasting than revenue-lead retrenchments. This is particularly true for the federal government, which has displayed a marked tendency in the past to engage in "tax and spend" behaviour. The fiscal retrenchments of the 1990s represents a market departure from the past.

4.5 Case Studies

In this section, we take a closer look at the fiscal policy choices made by three fiscal authorities; the federal government and the provincial governments of Alberta and Ontario. We chose these fiscal authorities because each presents a different aspect of the deficit and debt problem and the response to that problem. For each of these fiscal authorities we examine separately the revenue and expenditure impulses that make up the fiscal impulses. A separate examination reveals some detail of the *composition* of specific fiscal impulses. Thus, we are able to identify whether the fiscal impulses of a particular fiscal authority in a particular year were due mainly to revenue or expenditure changes. It will also be useful to examine whether our estimates of the discretionary impulses for a particular fiscal authority correspond to known policy changes as announced in budget papers, for this will provide another test of the reliability of our impulse estimates. Finally, we also present estimates of what we call the *cyclical impulse*. The cyclical impulse measures the change in the budget deficit arising from changes in the business cycle, holding the budgetary effects of policy changes constant. The sum of the cyclical and the fiscal impulse measure the total change in the primary deficit from the previous year. A comparison of the cyclical and the fiscal impulse reveals to what extent fiscal policy choices either complemented or offset changes in the budget deficit due to changes in economic conditions.

4.5.1 The Federal Government

The top graph in Figure 4-2 plots our measures of the fiscal and cyclical impulses for the federal government. Positive values of the fiscal impulse indicate an increase in the ratio of the primary deficit to GDP due to fiscal policy choices. Negative values indicate a reduction in the primary deficit/GDP ratio due to policy choices. Positive values of the cyclical impulse indicate an addition to the deficit due to changes in economic conditions. Negative values indicate a reduction in the deficit due to changes in economic conditions.

The influence of the business cycle on the federal budget is seen by movements of the cyclical impulse over time. Thus, the recessions in 1982/83, 1990/92, 1975/77, and 1970/71 – listed in order from most to least severe – show up as cyclical impulses that added 1.5, 1.4, 1.1 and 0.7 percentage points, respectively, to the federal government's deficit/GDP ratio. The years of solid economic growth from 1962 to 1966, and again from 1984 to 1989, show up as a series of negative cyclical impulses denoting annual cyclically-induced decreases in the federal primary deficit to GDP ratio. During these periods of strong economic growth, these negative cyclical impulses averaged about 0.3 percentage points.

Figure 4-2: Federal Government Impulses, 1962-96

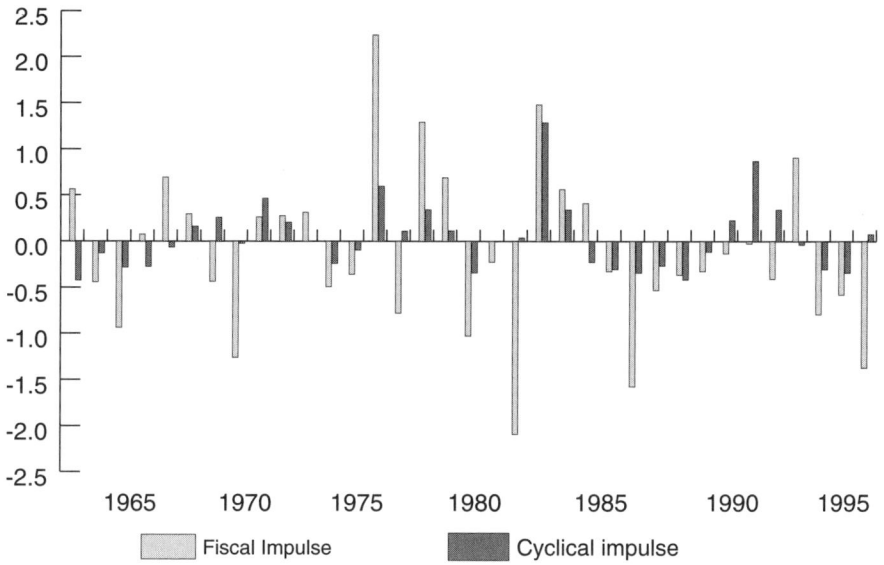

Fiscal Impulse   Cyclical impulse

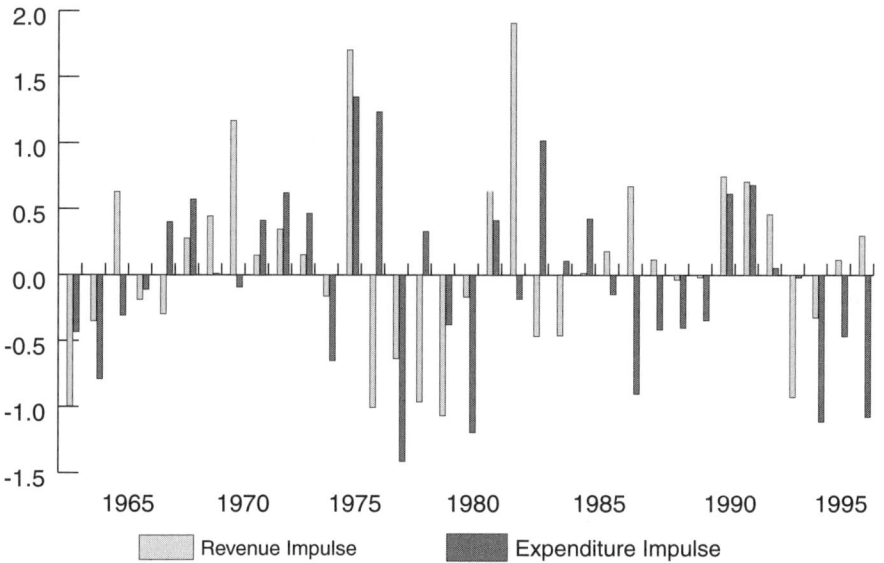

Revenue Impulse   Expenditure Impulse

The economic recovery beginning in 1993 produced reductions in the deficit in 1994 and 1995 before a small increase in the unemployment rate in 1996 produced a small cyclically-induced increase in the deficit.

Over the period 1962-96, the average discretionary fiscal impulse for the federal government was small (-0.13) and the federal government generally avoided large fiscal impulses of either sign. In fact, only one very loose stance (1975) and two very tight stances (1981 and 1986) were adopted over this period. Policy-induced reductions in the federal prima-ry deficit/GDP ratio (negative values for the fiscal impulse) were often introduced during periods of economic expansion. Similarly, policy-induced increases in the primary deficit to GDP ratio (positive fiscal impulses) were often introduced during periods of economic slowdowns. The federal government's fiscal and cyclical impulses moved in the same direction 62% of the time. This suggests that policy-induced reductions in the deficit/GDP ratio tended to be introduced during periods of rela-tive prosperity. Similarly, policy-induced increases in the deficit/GDP ratio tended to be introduced during periods of relative misery. Interestingly, the positive correlation of fiscal and cyclical impulses was less true of the provinces. The cyclical and fiscal impulses of the provinces moved in the same direction only 52% of the time.

The bottom graph in Figure 4-2 plots our measures of the revenue and expenditure impulses for the federal government. Positive values for the revenue and expenditure impulses indicate discretionary increases in tax revenue and program expenditures. Thus, a positive revenue impulse and a negative expenditure impulse each reduce the deficit. Revenue and expenditure impulses of the same sign are off-setting in their impact on the deficit.

A comparison of fiscal impulses with the revenue and expenditure impulses shows that small fiscal impulses were often the result of size-able, but offsetting, expenditure and revenue impulses. Thus, although the fiscal impulse in 1974 was small, the revenue and expenditure impulses show that this year was witness to a major expansion in the fed-eral budget in the form of substantial increases in both revenue and pro-gram expenditures. A similar pattern is observed in 1990 and 1991; years of small fiscal impulses that were the result of sizeable expenditure and revenue impulses that were offsetting in their impact on the deficit. This emphasizes yet again the bias of federal fiscal policy in favour of a grow-ing government.

Budget year 1966 is notable for marking a change from an earlier peri-od of mainly negative expenditure and revenue impulses to a period of mainly positive expenditure and revenue impulses. Thus, 1966 marked a change from the 1962-65 period when government's share of the economy – measured by program expenditures and by revenue as a fraction of GDP – was shrinking, to the 1967-72 period when government's share would steadily increase. Interestingly, however, both of these periods were characterized by roughly balanced budget changes in the federal budget; any expenditure impulse's impact on the budget was more or less offset by a revenue impulse of generally the same magnitude.

In 1975, this policy of introducing more or less balanced budget changes ended. In that year, a large, positive fiscal impulse was introduced due to a large positive expenditure impulse and a large negative revenue impulse. The revenue impulse was the result of a package of substantial tax cuts, including a three percentage point cut in the personal income tax rate, an accelerated write-off on purchases of capital equipment by businesses, the introduction of a $1,000 deduction for dividend and interest incomes and for private pension plans, and the introduction of a home savings program.[16] The expenditure impulse reflects the introduction in 1974 of measures that more than doubled business subsidies and capital assistance, an increase equal to 6% of total federal spending in that year.

Figure 4-2 shows that the federal government's first (of two) very tight stance in our sample period, in 1981, was due almost solely to a very large, positive, revenue impulse. That revenue impulse corresponded to the substantial increase in federal tax revenues as a result of the introduction of the National Energy Program. New revenues added $3 billion to federal revenues that had totalled $45 billion in the previous year. This increase in revenue, combined with a small decrease in GDP due to the early effects on the 1982/83 recession, combined to produce a revenue impulse equal to 1.9 percentage points of GDP. Thus, one of only two very tight stances introduced by the federal government during our sample period came as a result of a huge revenue grab from oil-producing provinces.

The only other example of a very tight stance introduced by the federal government over our sample period occurred in 1986. This stance, equal to 1.6% of GDP, differed from the 1981 stance in that it was the product of sizeable negative expenditure impulse and almost equally large positive revenue impulse. These policy choices can be traced to the first budget of the newly elected (in November 1984) Mulroney government. The positive revenue impulse was due to a number of tax increases, including the partial de-indexing of income taxes, the application of two income surtaxes, and the end of the home ownership savings plan. Taken together, these measures would add over $5 billion to a revenue base of $77 billion in 1986. On the spending side, the budget phased out the Petroleum Incentive Program, announced the sale of a number of Crown corporations, and substantially reduced grants and subsidies. For the first time, the federal government also raised the issue of cutting transfers to the provinces and, more importantly politically, proposed to partially de-index old age pensions. This last policy proposal proved to be an important one because it created a political furor that would put a chill on further efforts to introduce cuts to social programs as a way of reducing the deficit.[17]

The next two years of the first Mulroney mandate, and the first year of the second, produced three negative expenditure impulses with insignificant revenue impulses. In the last three years of the second Mulroney mandate, 1990 to 1992 inclusive, while fiscal impulses remained negative, their composition changed considerably. Whereas in the previous four years the negative impulses were due almost solely to expenditure cuts, in the next three years negative fiscal impulses of the same general magnitude were now the result of large, positive revenue impulses offset by slightly smaller positive expenditure impulses. Thus, in the last three years of its second mandate, the Mulroney government introduced discretionary policy changes that increased the size of government's share of GDP. Election year 1993 produced the only discretionary increase in the deficit during the Mulroney regime; a deficit increase due to a substantial negative revenue impulse.

The attack on the federal deficit by the newly elected Liberal government began in earnest with the budget presented in the spring of 1993. As Figure 4-2 shows, this budget introduced changes that resulted in a large negative expenditure impulse in the following year. In 1995 and 1996, two more negative expenditure impulses followed, this time supported by positive revenue impulses. The sum of these three fiscal impulses was -2.74 percentage points of GDP. Thus the improvement in the federal primary budget balance that saw it increase from a surplus of 0.8% of GDP in 1993 to a surplus equal to 4.1% of GDP in 1997 – an improvement equal to 3.3 percentage points of GDP – was mainly due to discretionary budgetary choices. In particular, the improvement was due to cuts to program expenditures. As we noted previously, a large portion of these expenditure cuts were cuts to the grants the federal government sends to the provinces. These cuts amounted to 1.0 percentage point of GDP from 1993-96. Thus, of the total improvement to the federal primary surplus of 3.3 percentage points of GDP, 1.0 percentage point was due to cuts to provincial grants, and 1.7 percentage points was due to cuts to other federal spending programs and policy-induced increases in revenues. The remaining 0.6 percentage points was due to improvements in the economy and the effects of automatic stabilizers. Thus, only about half of the improvement in the federal deficit to GDP ratio can be attributed to non-transfer related policy changes.

PAST (IN)DISCRETIONS

The eleven years from 1986 to 1996, inclusive, is an interesting period of history in the federal government's efforts to control its deficit. Throughout this period, high interest rates, combined with a large outstanding debt, drove the federal government's debt servicing costs ever higher. Just to maintain a more or less constant deficit to GDP ratio would require discretionary policy actions. Discretionary policy changes concentrated on expenditure cuts with the exception of the period 1990 to 1992, a period of sizeable positive expenditure impulses accompanied by positive revenue impulses. The fact that this period corresponded to the last years of an unpopular Conservative government and the prelude to an election in 1993 suggests the possibility that political considerations had an important role to play in determining budget choices. We return to this issue in Chapter 5.

4.5.2 The Government of Ontario

Figure 4-3 presents our estimates of the fiscal, cyclical, revenue, and expenditure impulses for the province of Ontario. Again, the business cycle reveals itself in Ontario's cyclical impulses. By comparing Ontario's cyclical impulses to those from the federal budget, we see that in Ontario the 1991 recession was somewhat more severe than the 1982 recession, whereas the opposite was true for Canada as a whole. It is also apparent that the recession hit Ontario earlier than it did the rest of the country; in 1989 Ontario's cyclical impulse turned positive (indicating a business cycle-induced increase in the deficit) while the federal government was still enjoying a negative cycle impulse.[18] For the most part, however, the movements of Ontario's cyclical impulses of the time closely resemble those of the federal government. This is not surprising, of course, since the Ontario economy makes up about 40% of the Canadian economy.

The Ontario government's fiscal, revenue, and expenditure impulses during the 1960s exhibit a remarkable pattern. Although fiscal impulses were generally small in the 1960s, the bottom graph shows this was a period of very rapid growth in the provincial government's share of the Ontario economy. Expenditure impulses were, with the exception of 1964, consistently large and positive, averaging just under 0.7 percentage points of GDP. Largely due to these discretionary policy choices, the Ontario government increased its ratio of program expenditures to GDP from 7.9% in 1962 to 13.1% in 1970. Over this same period, however, revenue impulses were also consistently large and positive, averaging just over 0.7 percentage points of GDP. Largely as a result of discretionary policy choices, then, the ratio of revenues to GDP increased from 8.4% in 1962 to 13.7% in 1970. During the 1960s while the provincial govern-

Figure 4-3: Ontario Government Impulses, 1962-96

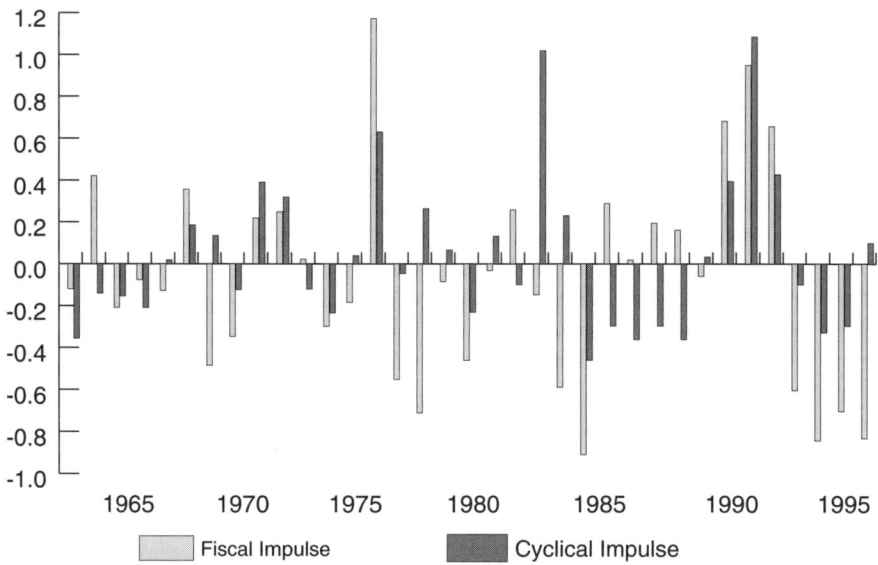

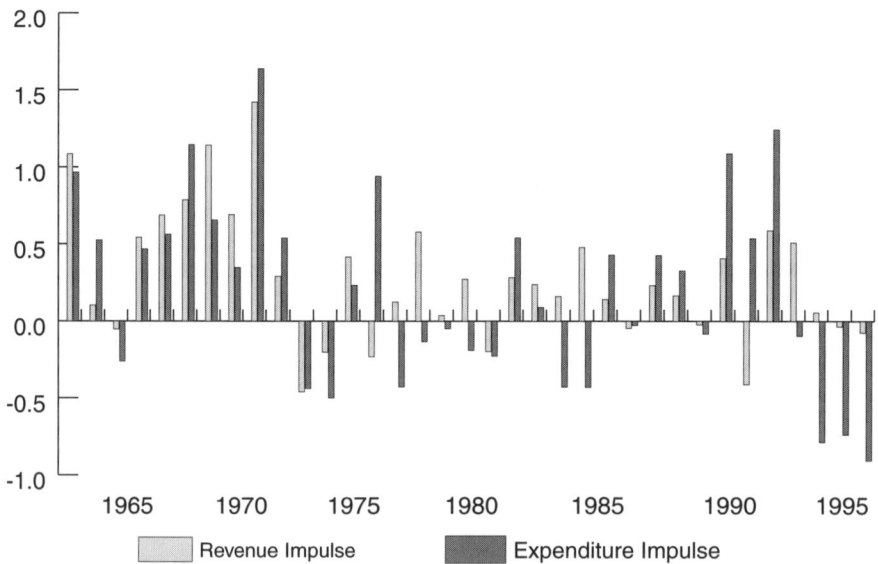

PAST (IN)DISCRETIONS

ment sector grew quite dramatically, the deficit to GDP ratio was not very much affected by discretionary policy choices. During this period, and indeed for most of its history since 1961, the government of Ontario has displayed very prudent fiscal policy behaviour.

From 1970 to 1989, the government of Ontario rarely introduced any sizeable revenue, expenditure or fiscal impulses. Indeed, over the 1962-96 period, Ontario did not adopt a single very tight or very loose fiscal stance. The largest of Ontario's non-neutral stances came in 1975 and 1984 when discretionary changes in the deficit equal to +1.2% and -0.9% of provincial GDP were introduced, respectively. Contributing to the 1975 stance was a temporary cut in the provincial sales tax from 7% to 5%, a temporary exemption of car purchases from the sales tax and a cut in succession duties.[19] The other large stance, by Ontario standards, that occurred in 1984 was the result of revenue and expenditure impulses that, while relatively small, were opposite in sign and so had a relatively large effect on the budget deficit.

Drama returned to Ontario's budget history with the election of an NDP government in 1990. That election coincides with three successive positive fiscal impulses each of which added to the previous year's deficit. As the top graph shows, these fiscal impulses were introduced during a period when a serious recession was producing large and positive cyclical impulses. This pattern reflects the effort of the government to adopt a counter-cyclical fiscal policy to mitigate the effects of the recession that struck Ontario in the year it was elected. The positive fiscal and cyclical impulses, which when summed together measure the change in the observed deficit to GDP ratio, produced a rapid increase in Ontario's deficit and its debt/GDP ratio. Indeed, by 1993, when Ontario was beginning to recover from recession, the debt/GDP ratio had grown from 11% in 1989/90 to 20% in 1992/93.

The bottom graph in Figure 4-3 shows that the large fiscal impulses observed over the 1990-92 period were mainly due to discretionary increases in program spending. In an effort to halt the growth in the deficit, the government introduced a "social contract" with public sector employees in 1993. This initiative, which cut $2 billion from the public payroll, introduced a significant negative expenditure impulse in 1994 and began a period of expenditure cuts that would continue to the end of our sample period. Discretionary revenue changes were also introduced by the NDP government to try and halt the growth in the deficit. In 1993 the personal income tax rate was increased from 53% to 58% of the federal rate and a high income surtax was introduced. Together, these measures produced two consecutive negative fiscal impulses in the final two years of the NDP government. In fact, the negative fiscal impulse in

1994, at 0.94% of GDP, was the second largest effort at deficit reduction in Ontario during our sample period.

In 1995, the Conservative government of Mike Harris was elected in Ontario. Harris had campaigned on a platform of cuts to both program expenditure and tax rates. The cuts to program expenditures are clearly identified in the bottom graph by large, negative expenditure impulses in 1995 and 1996. The well-known cuts to the personal income tax rate in Ontario did not begin until the 1996 tax year when the personal income tax rate was cut from 58% to 56% of the federal rate. The larger cuts, that are scheduled to reduced it to 38.5% of the federal rate by July 1, 1999, do not show up in our data.

Just as we found in reviewing the recent history of the federal government's budgeting behaviour, we see signs that politics played an important role in determining fiscal policy choices in Ontario. The "province-building" goal of the Conservative government of John Robarts (1961-71) is evident by the large, positive expenditure impulses during the 1960s. However, that same government's fiscal conservatism is also evident from the large, positive revenue impulses. Thus, the province-building exercise was financed without resort to a large build-up in debt. These policy choices stand in stark contrast to the choices made by the NDP government of Bob Rae (1990-95). In the first three years of that government's mandate, increases in program expenditures were financed mainly by borrowing. When the consequences of that choice for the province's debt to GDP ratio became apparent, large cuts to program expenditures and large tax increases were introduced in the final two years of the mandate. Thus fiscal policy choices differed significantly by governing political party and, in the case of the NDP government, differed significantly between the first and second half of the mandate.

4.5.3 The Government of Alberta

Figure 4-4 presents the fiscal, cyclical, revenue and expenditure impulses emanating from the budget of the province of Alberta. Note, first of all, the difference in scale in these plots from those in Figures 4-2 and 4-3. The Alberta economy and the government of Alberta's budget have both experienced significantly more volatility than has been the case in either Ontario or in Canada as a whole. This is not surprising given the Alberta economy's reliance on the oil and gas industry, the Alberta government's at times heavy reliance on energy royalties, and often volatile world energy prices.

A comparison of the cyclical impulse in Alberta with that in Ontario highlights the uniqueness of Alberta's business cycle.[20] Thus, for example, Alberta enjoyed a string of cyclically- induced deficit reductions from 1973 to 1978, inclusive, due to rising world oil prices. During the same

Figure 4-4: Alberta Government Impulses, 1962-96

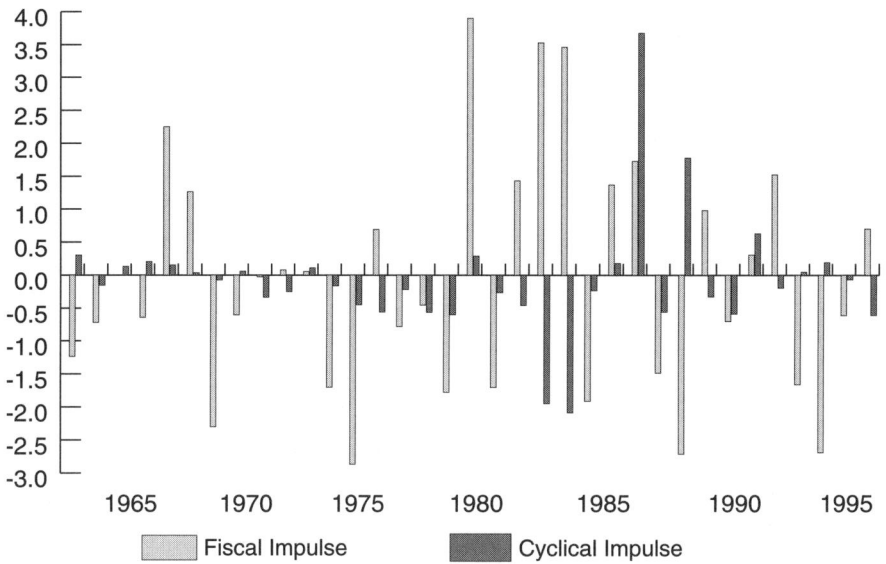

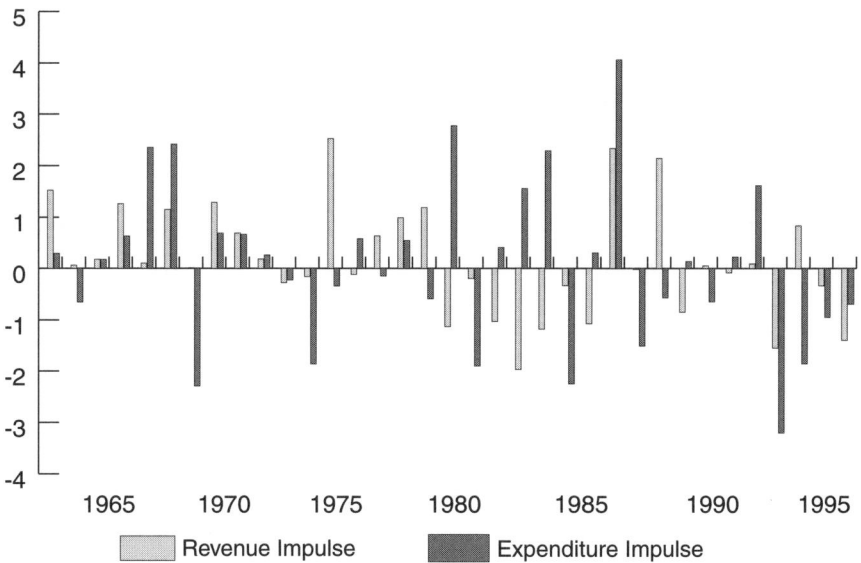

Fiscal Impulse Cyclical Impulse

Revenue Impulse Expenditure Impulse

period, Ontario was realizing cyclically-induced deficit increases for the same reason. Similarly, the recession that struck hard in Ontario during the 1990-93 period affected Alberta much less severely.

Energy prices have historically played a key role in determining Alberta's budget choices. The first OPEC oil price shock saw the Edmonton price of crude oil increase from $2.90 per barrel in 1972 to $3.50 in 1973 and $5.80 in 1974.[21] In response, the Alberta government quickly introduced legislation to increase its share of energy rents in 1973 by tying royalties to the international price of oil. Royalty rates were increased again in 1974 and over the next few years a series of provincial and federal government actions increased the Canadian price of energy and the royalty rates applied against this price.[22] As a result, Alberta benefited from a series of positive revenue impulses during the mid 1970s that added 2.8 percentage points to the provincial revenue to GDP ratio.

The largest of Alberta's fiscal impulses was a positive fiscal impulse in 1979. This impulse corresponds to the province's municipal debt reduction program.[23] That program alone increased the province's spending in that year by 40%, a discretionary spending change shown by the large, positive expenditure impulse in the bottom diagram. In the same year, a negative revenue impulse resulted from a large corporation income tax cut. Together, these policy changes resulted in what we calculate to have been a discretionary increase in Alberta's deficit equal to almost 4% of provincial GDP.

The years 1981 to 1986 marked an important and volatile period in Alberta's recent economic history. In October 1980, the federal government introduced the National Energy Program (NEP). The NEP increased the federal government's share of energy royalties, decreased the Alberta government's share, and increased Canadian ownership of the oil and gas industry. Most importantly for the Alberta government's budget position, the announcement of the NEP caused a massive shift of investment out of the province and a dramatic downturn in the fortunes of oil and gas companies. In response, the government introduced a number of measures to counteract this withdrawal of investment. Thus 1982 saw the introduction of the Alberta Economic Resurgence Plan which took steps to lighten the royalty burden on oil and gas firms and led to a substantial increase in provincial government spending designed to benefit the stricken oil and gas industry, to reduce interest costs, and to increase education spending. During this period, then, the province introduced measures that yielded both positive expenditure impulses and negative revenue impulses. The combination of these yielded very large positive fiscal impulses over the 1981-83 period.

It is interesting to note that over this same 1981-83 period, the cyclical impulses were large and negative, indicating that the influence of the business cycle on the deficit, after accounting for the effects of the NEP and government policy measures in response to it, was toward a lower deficit. These cyclical impulses reflect the fact that oil prices continued to climb over this period. If not for the deleterious effects of the NEP, then, rising oil prices would have generated reductions in Alberta's deficit (or, more precisely, increases in the provincial government's surplus).

Over our sample period, the largest cyclically-induced decline in the Alberta government's budget position occurred in 1986. This was the result of a collapse in oil prices that saw the Edmonton price fall from $34.50 in 1985 to $18.85 in 1986. A slight recovery in oil prices (to $22.60) in 1987 generated a small negative cyclical impulse (denoting an improvement in the budget position) but this was followed by a second fall in prices (to $16.70) in the next year. The 1986 collapse in oil prices caused the government to halt resource royalty contributions to the Alberta Heritage Fund, prompted an increase in the personal income tax rate of three percentage points, added a flat tax and a surtax on personal income, and increased the corporate income tax rate. These policy changes are represented by the large and positive revenue impulse in 1986. Expenditures also increased significantly in 1986; the government introduced significant increases in support for farmers and livestock producers as well as a major incentive program for the oil and gas sector. The net effect of this discretionary increase in expenditures and revenues was a positive fiscal impulse. Thus both fiscal policy and the business cycle caused a worsening in the budget balance with the result that the Alberta government realized a very large total budget deficit.

The arrival of Ralph Klein as Premier in the fall of 1992 marked a turn-around in Alberta's budgetary policies. Klein was elected on a platform of making a 20% cut to program expenditures. As promised, these cuts began with the 1993 budget. As the bottom graph in Figure 4-4 shows, the cuts were front-loaded, with smaller cuts coming in each of the next three years. What's more, it is clear that cuts to expenditures were the main source of Alberta's improved deficit record over this period. Revenue increases were relatively minor and the economy contributed relatively little to the improvement in the primary deficit prior to 1996.

The pattern of discretionary fiscal impulses in Alberta is interesting in part because it highlights two distinct periods in the province's finances; a revenue-abundant period of high and growing oil and gas prices and a booming economy during the 1970s, and a revenue-short period following the second OPEC price shock in 1979, the NEP, and the 1986 collapse in oil prices. During the revenue-abundant period, the province introduced changes to the energy royalty system that produced reductions in the deficit (or, more accurately during this period, increases in the provincial surplus) despite a program of rapid growth in provincial spending under the direction of governments led by Peter Lougheed. During this period, revenue policy was very counter-cyclical and led to the growth of the Alberta Heritage Savings Trust Fund. Expenditure policy, however, was very pro-cyclical as Lougheed aggressively expanded the public sector. The net effect was counter-cyclical thanks to the huge revenue gains over this period. The revenue-short period was dominated by discretionary policies that added to the deficit; the policies described above as efforts to cushion the impact of the NEP and the 1982 recession. During this period, provincial spending was generally counter-cyclical while revenues fluctuated widely with swings in energy prices.

Politics, of course, appear to have played an important role in determining fiscal policy choices in Alberta. Doern and Toner argue that to analyse the NEP only in terms of economic policy is to fundamentally misunderstand its origins and its nature.[24] Paul Boothe's interview study with key decision-makers in the Alberta government during the 1968-91 period confirms this judgement. These decision-makers, who included former Premiers and former Treasurers, recognized the existence of an election cycle in spending, though they denied its importance.[25] Certainly, the election that brought Ralph Klein to power in 1992 also produced a very important change in economic policy.

4.5.4 The Rest
To conclude this chapter, we present, in Figure 4-5, the revenue and expenditure impulses for the remaining eight fiscal authorities. While we won't discuss these in detail, a few points are worth noting.

The revenue and expenditure impulses in Newfoundland and PEI are notable for their large size. As discussed previously, this principally reflects the large share of the government sector in those provinces. It is also noteworthy that over our sample period, expenditure impulses have grown smaller in these provinces. This is especially true in PEI where discretionary policies were quite small during the late 1980s and early 1990s before a concerted effort at deficit reduction via cuts to program spending was commenced upon.

Nova Scotia's impulses identify a clear change in policy in 1981. Before that date, expenditure impulses were typically positive (adding to the deficit) whereas afterward the opposite was true. Although the same political party (Conservative) and the same Premier (Buchanan) governed the province from 1978 to 1990, clearly a change in fiscal policy direction was adopted in 1981.

Figure 4-5: Revenue and Expenditure Impulses, 1962-96
Newfoundland

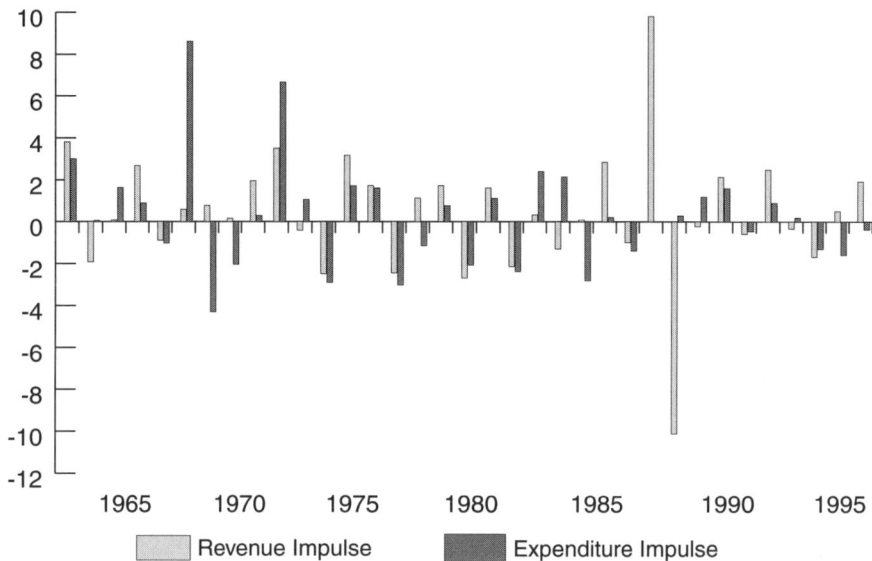

Revenue Impulse   Expenditure Impulse

Prince Edward Island

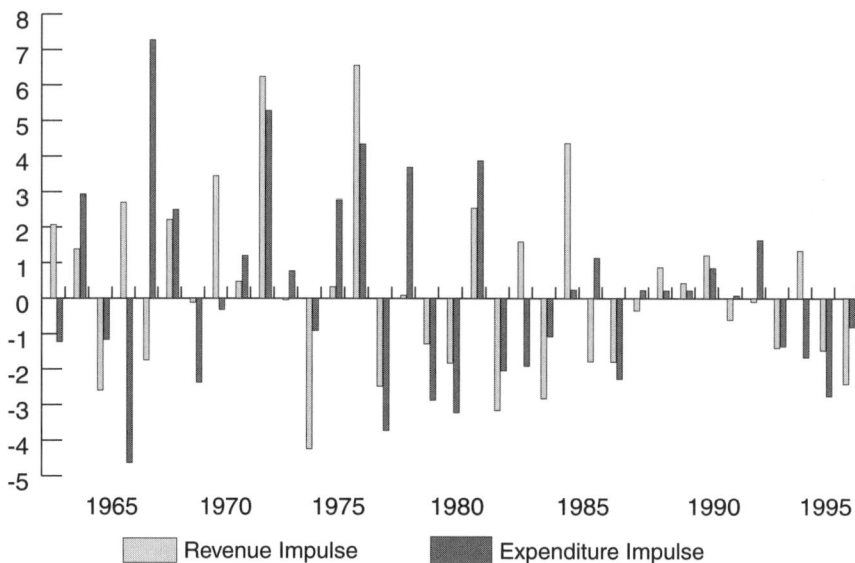

Revenue Impulse   Expenditure Impulse

Nova Scotia

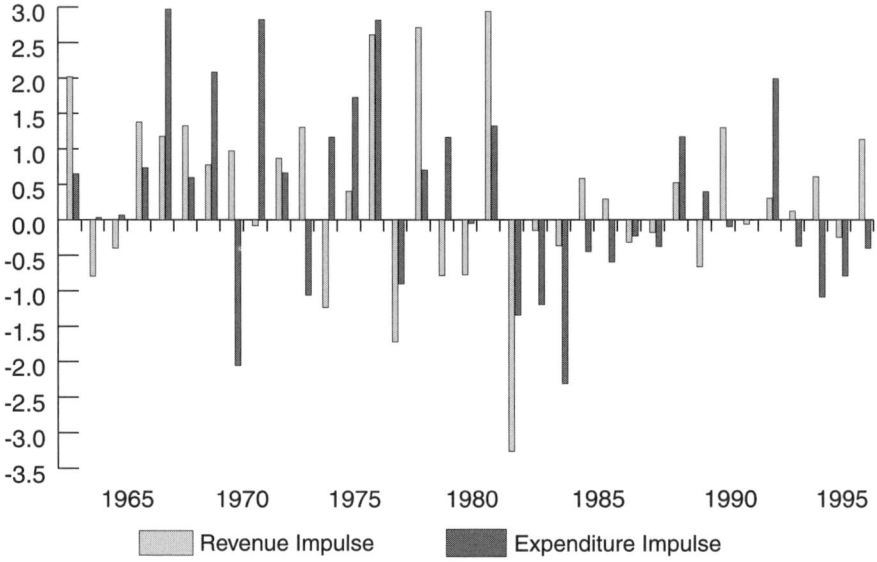

Revenue Impulse   Expenditure Impulse

New Brunswick

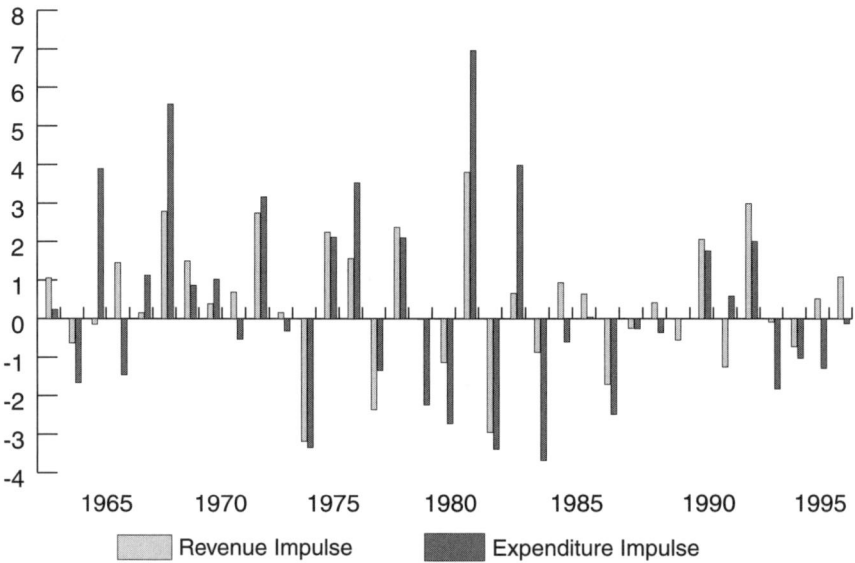

Revenue Impulse   Expenditure Impulse

Quebec

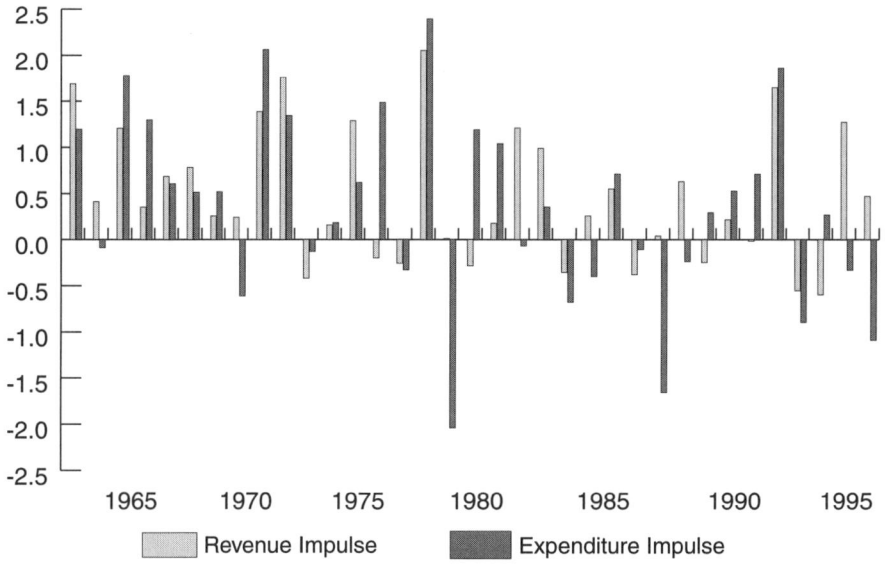

Revenue Impulse   Expenditure Impulse

Manitoba

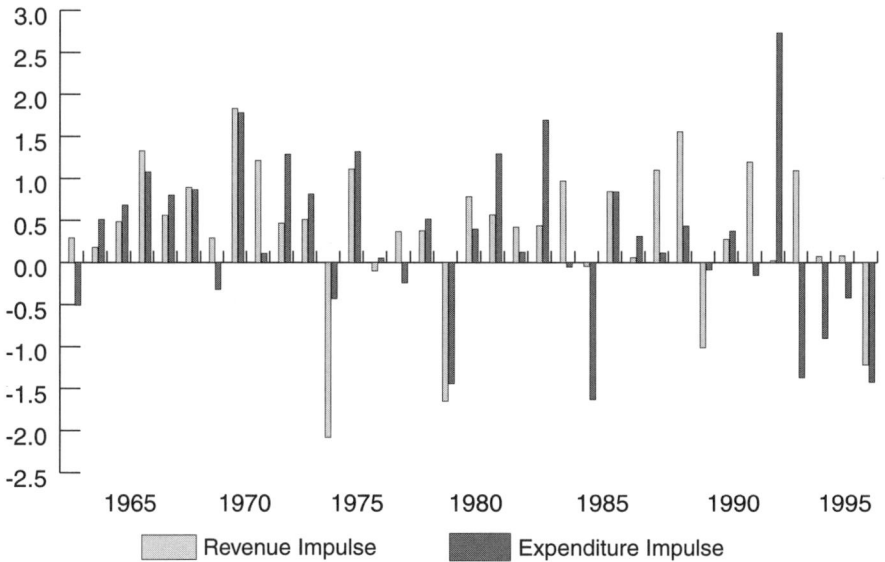

Revenue Impulse   Expenditure Impulse

Saskatchewan

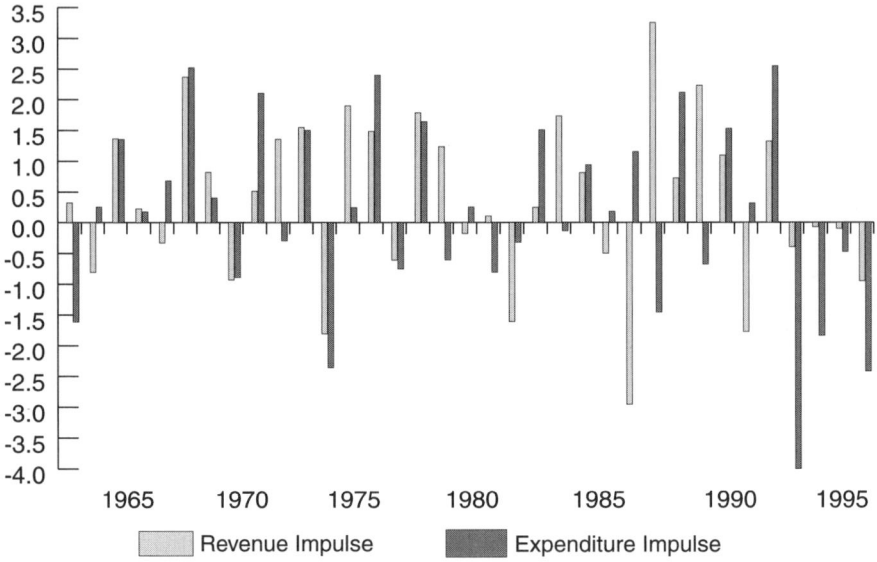

Revenue Impulse   Expenditure Impulse

British Columbia

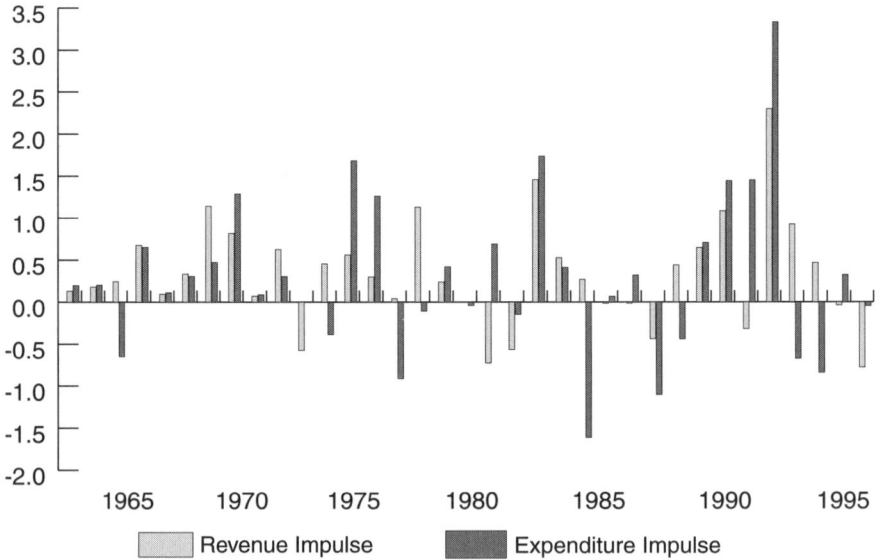

Revenue Impulse   Expenditure Impulse

The government of New Brunswick seems also to have experienced a change in fiscal policy direction, though not until the mid 1980s. It is interesting that around this time a long period of governments ruling with only small majorities came to an end when, in 1982, a Conservative and then, in 1987, a Liberal government ruled with large majorities.

Like Ontario, the impulses in Quebec define a period of more or less balanced budget growth of the provincial government sector during the 1960s. In contrast with Ontario, the last two observations for Quebec, 1995 and 1996, show that deficit reduction in that province has relied as heavily on revenue increases as expenditure cuts.

Manitoba's impulses are notable for the fact that until 1993 the great majority of impulses were positive. Thus fiscal policy has been to increase the provincial government's share of the economy but to do so with tax-financed expenditure increases. From 1993 to 1996, the Manitoba government imposed four large negative expenditure impulses in an effort to balance its budget.

The seriousness of the debt crisis in Saskatchewan is apparent from the very large negative expenditure impulses in 1993, 1994 and 1996. This response is all the more remarkable because it was an NDP government that imposed these cuts.

Finally, expenditure and revenue impulses in British Columbia have typically been small. Prolonged periods of very small impulses during the late 1970s and mid 1980s are worth remarking upon as this non-interventionist philosophy has not been often observed elsewhere in Canada. It is also interesting to note the parallels between the policies of the NDP governments in British Columbia (1991-96) and in Ontario (1990-95). Both began their mandate with sizeable increases in program spending to be followed, in the latter half of their mandate, with large expenditure cuts.

Appendix 4-1

This appendix describes the method employed to derived estimates of $R^*(t)$ and $E^*(t)$ for each of our eleven fiscal authorities.

We estimated, using ordinary least squares, for each fiscal authority, two regressions of the following form;

$$E(t) = a_0 + a_1 TS + a_2 UR(t) + e(t)$$
$$R(t) = \beta_0 + \beta_1 TR + \beta_2 UR(t) + \mu(t)$$

where $E(t)$ = program spending as a fraction of GDP in year t, $R(t)$ = tax revenue as a fraction of GDP in year t, TR and TE = trend variables whose definition we discuss below, $UR(t)$ = the provincial (national, for the federal government) unemployment rate in period t, and where e and μ are error terms. We then used the estimated coefficients to generate the level of program spending (E(t)*) and tax revenue (R(t)*) in period t which would have occurred had the unemployment rate remained at the level it was last period;

$$E(t)^* = \hat{a}_0 + \hat{a}_1 TS + \hat{a}_2 UR(t\text{-}1) + \hat{e}(t)$$
$$R(t)^* = \hat{\beta}_0 + \hat{\beta}_1 TR + \hat{\beta}_2 UR(t\text{-}1) + \hat{\mu}(t)$$

Using these estimates of E(t)* and R(t)*, we calculated the expenditure, revenue, and fiscal impulses in the manner described in the text.

Alesina and Perotti (1995) use two linear trends (for periods 1960-75 and 1976-92) in their regressions of E(t) and R(t) on unemployment rates. They do so in order to account for a change in the trend rates of growth in the spending and tax revenue series. It is apparent in our data too, that the trend rate of growth in these series changed over our estimation period (1961-95). However, the date at which the change in these trend rates of growth differs by province, by level of government and is different for spending versus revenues. In recognition of this, we defined TE and TR as government-specific, non-linear trends derived by applying the Hodrick-Prescott filter to E(t) and R(t) respectively. Because the use of the Hodrick-Prescott filter can introduce cycles into time series, we experimented with linear trends and linear trends with breaks. Our results did not prove to be very sensitive to these alternative specifications.

To accommodate the fact that energy royalties make up a large fraction of Alberta's revenues (in 1978, for example, natural resource revenue made up 60% of provincial revenues), Alberta's revenue equation includes the real price of oil (OIL) as a regressor and uses two linear trends (1961-84, 1985-95). Thus the revenue/GDP ratio that Alberta would have realized in period t had economic conditions remained the same as in period t-1 was determined by calculating;

$$R(t)^* = \hat{\beta}_0 + \hat{\beta}_1 TREND1 + \hat{\beta}_2 TREND2 + \hat{\beta}_3 UR(t\text{-}1) + \hat{\beta}_4 OIL(t\text{-}1) + \hat{\mu}(t)$$

where the estimated coefficients came from a similar regression involving UR(t) and OIL(t).

Data on provincial unemployment rates are available from the CANSIM data base for the years 1966 to the present. As well as these data, we have made use of provincial unemployment rate data covering the years 1961-65 inclusive. These data have been constructed using labour force and employment data available from issues of the *Canadian Statistical Review*. Details on the construction of these data are available from the authors on request.

CHAPTER FIVE

POLITICS AND FISCAL
POLICY IN CANADA

In the review of fiscal policies presented in the previous chapter, we have seen some signs that politics may have played an important role in the fiscal policy choices of Canadian governments. There is, of course, little doubt that political considerations play an important role in fiscal policy-making. As noted recently by Avinash Dixit,

> In reality, a policy proposal is merely the beginning of a process that is *political* at every stage – not merely the process of legislation, but also the implementation, including the choice or formation of an administrative agency and the subsequent operation of the agency. (Dixit (1996), page 9)

In this chapter, we will examine some aspects of this question directly, by investigating to what extent fiscal policy choices in Canada are correlated with the timing of elections and the preferences of the governing political party.

The political process is generally thought to influence policy choices in at least two fundamental ways.[1] The first arises from the desire on the part of incumbent parties to be re-elected. To signal to voters their competence as policy-makers, elected officials may introduce policies that are different from choices that would be introduced if an election was not soon to follow. These "opportunistic" responses of policy-makers to the timing of elections are an attempt to curry favour with voters and thus increase their likelihood of re-election. The political process may also influence policy choices via so-called "partisan" effects. The idea here is that political parties differ in their opinions regarding appropriate policy choices and they seek election in order to implement those policies. Thus, changes in the governing party will also result in changes in policy choices.

To investigate whether opportunistic and/or partisan influences exist in fiscal policy, it is necessary to control for changes in the business cycle. This is because opportunistic and partisan influences, if they exist, will manifest themselves in the discretionary choices made by governments. Thus, it is necessary to separate changes in government revenues and expenditures due to changes in economic conditions from those due to discretionary changes in economic policy; that is, changes in tax rates and spending propensities. In most studies that look at opportunistic and partisan cycles in fiscal policy, this is accomplished by estimating a pooled time series, cross-section regression of revenues and expenditures on measures of the economic cycle as well as on measures intended to capture opportunistic and partisan effects. The measures of the economic cycle "control" for changes in economic conditions and thus remove the influence of changes in economic conditions from government revenues and expenditures. In this way, the variables measuring opportunistic and partisan effects are correlated against changes in revenues and expenditures that arise solely due to changes in policy. An implicit assumption of this approach is that the budgets of all the governments included in the study are equally sensitive to changes in economic conditions.[2]

The approach we use to investigate the existence of opportunistic and partisan effects differs from this approach in a number of ways. First, we use estimates of fiscal policy changes that have already been purged of cyclical influences via the calculation of fiscal impulses described above. There is, then, no need to include measures of the business cycle in our regressions. We view this as an improvement over the approach taken in the literature because that approach requires using estimates of potential output (or a measure of the "natural" rate of unemployment). The problem here is that values of potential output are unobserved and are not constant, either across time or across economic jurisdictions. Thus, measures of the business cycle are difficult to determine. As we noted in section 4.1, Blanchard's method for calculating fiscal impulses avoids this difficulty. A second way our approach differs from that taken in the literature is that we do not impose the assumption that the budgets of all governments included in the study are equally sensitive to changes in economic conditions. We judge this to be important because Kneebone and McKenzie (1998) present evidence that this is simply an inappropriate assumption for Canadian governments. By first removing the cyclical influence from our data with the use of province-specific regressions (as described in Chapter 4), we avoid that restrictive assumption.

The results presented in this chapter contribute to this literature by investigating the potential for opportunistic and partisan influences on discretionary changes in expenditures and revenues of sub-national governments. We suspect that the fiscal policy choices of national governments have been prevalent in this literature because most country's sub-national governments do not have sufficient budget flexibility to enable them to manipulate their budgets in response to political considerations. Many state governments in the United States, for example, are constrained by balanced budget legislation. Canadian provinces, however, have not been so constrained during our sample period. What's more, as we saw in Chapter 2, the expenditure responsibilities of Canadian provinces, and their access to a wide variety of revenue sources, is on par with most national governments.

To obtain a sufficiently large number of observations on opportunistic and partisan effects, it is generally necessary to pool data across governments. When this is done across national economies, an important problem arises. A further set of control variables becomes necessary to account for differences across countries in exchange rates, monetary policy, and government and electoral institutions.[3] These factors are difficult to control for and any attempt to do so will necessarily be imperfect. Indeed, it is often the case that no attempt is made to control for these influences at all. By using Canadian provincial and federal government data, we avoid the need to include such variables because all governments in Canada are subject to the effects of the same monetary policy, the same degree of exchange rate intervention, and, of course, operate under the same electoral system and same parliamentary system of government. Thus, we are able to control for these influences in a way that is not possible to do in multi-country studies.

For this investigation, we use a panel of 385 observations on fiscal, expenditure and revenue impulses generated by Canada's eleven fiscal authorities over a period of 35 years (1962-96). Regressions were estimated relating these impulses to dummy variables identifying election years (ELECTION) and identifying governments from the left of the Canadian political spectrum (LEFT). Our sample contains 108 election years and 277 non-election years. We have defined "left-wing" governments as being Liberal, New Democrat, and Parti Quebecois governments; consequently, Progressive Conservative, Social Credit and Union Nationale governments are defined as "right-wing". Our sample contains 184 observations of left-wing governments and 201 observations of right-wing governments.[4] LEFT has been defined in such a way that it identifies the political party in power when the election is called (rather than the party that wins the election).

We also include a measure of the size of debt servicing costs as a fraction of total expenditures (INTEREST). This variable will increase due to both increases in the interest rate and increases in the level of debt. Thus, INTEREST measures the influence on current fiscal policy choices of current monetary policy and of past fiscal and monetary policy choices that caused debt to accumulate. We are particularly interested in whether increases in debt service costs "crowd out" program expenditures or "crowd in" revenues. Table 5-1 presents the results of our regressions.

Table 5-1: Political Influences on Fiscal Policy Choices, 1962-96

Dependent Variable	Fiscal Impulse	Expenditure Impulse	Revenue Impulse
CONSTANT	-0.13	-0.09	0.31
	(0.06)*	(0.07)	(0.05)*
ELECTION	0.41	0.31	-0.18
	(0.08)*	(0.07)*	(0.08)*
LEFT	0.11	0.25	0.06
	(0.06)†	(0.05)*	(0.05)
INTEREST	-0.30	-0.23	-0.07
	(0.04)*	(0.03)*	(0.03)*
$\overline{R}^2$	0.19	0.14	0.07
Durbin-Watson	2.08	2.16	2.46

Values in parentheses represent standard errors of the estimated coefficients. An asterisk denotes a coefficient whose value is significantly different from zero at the 5% level or better. A dagger denotes a coefficient whose value is significantly different from zero at the 10% level or better. Each of these regressions also included a first order autoregressive term. Each column presents results from a pooled regression based on 363 observations. The mean of the fiscal impulse is -0.10, the mean of the expenditure impulse is 0.21, and the mean of the revenue impulse is 0.31.

The constant term in these regressions measures the average fiscal, expenditure, and revenue impulse associated with a right-wing government (that is, a Progressive Conservative, Social Credit, or Union Nationale government) in a non-election year. Focussing initially on the first column in the table, our estimates indicate that, controlling for changes due to debt service costs, right-wing governments implemented discretionary *reductions* in the primary deficit in non-election years of 0.13 percentage points of GDP on average. The coefficient on the ELECTION variable measures the *difference* between the discretionary fiscal impulses of right-wing governments in election and non-election years. Election calls are associated with an average fiscal impulse that is significantly larger (by 0.41 percentage points of GDP) than that realized in non-election years. More specifically, in election years, right-wing governments implemented discretionary *increases* in the primary deficit averaging 0.28 percentage points of GDP (0.41-0.13), compared to the average 0.13 *decrease* in non- election years. This is reflective of a very strong opportunistic cycle in Canadian fiscal policy, wherein governments increase spending in election years and decrease spending in non-election years.

Still focussing on the first column, the coefficient on the LEFT variable indicates the presence of partisan effects on the fiscal policy choices of Canadian governments. Left-wing governments are associated with a fiscal impulse that is 0.11 percentage points larger than the (negative) fiscal impulse associated with right-wing governments.

To put the results from the first column in perspective, if the Liberal (left-wing by our definition) federal government had called an election in 1996, and had they acted as Canadian governments have acted (on average) in the past, our estimates suggest that the primary deficit would have increased by about $3.2 billion.

We have established the presence of strong opportunistic and partisan influences in Canadian fiscal policy. An interesting question is whether these influences tend to manifest themselves on the expenditure or the revenue side of the budget. This question is investigated in the second and third columns of Table 5-1.

The coefficient on the ELECTION variable indicates opportunistic influences on both expenditure and revenue impulses. The coefficient is interpreted as measuring the change in program spending and tax revenue collected in elections years *relative to what is observed in non-election years*. Thus, while in non-election years, program spending was decreased by an average of 0.09 percentage points of GDP, in election years program spending increased by an average of 0.22 percentage points of GDP (-0.09 + 0.31). Similarly, while in non-election years tax revenue increased by an average of 0.31 percentage points of GDP, in election years revenue still increased, but by a much smaller 0.13 percentage points of GDP (0.31 - 0.18). Interestingly, the impact of elections on the discretionary expenditure impulse is somewhat larger. This suggests that Canadian governments have tended to seek re-election through increases in program spending rather than by reducing the size of tax increases. This choice may be because governments can more easily target expenditures to specific groups and therefore score greater "political points" through spending increases.

Moving to the coefficient on the LEFT variable in the expenditure and revenue impulse columns, it is interesting to note now that partisan effects have tended to be confined to differences in expenditure policy rather than revenue policy - the coefficient on the LEFT variable is significantly different from zero only for discretionary expenditures.

The INTEREST variable measures the influence on fiscal policy choices of a change in debt servicing costs. Changes in INTEREST are due to changes in interest rates and changes in the level of outstanding debt. Our estimates indicate that increases in debt servicing costs are associated with reductions in the deficit/GDP ratio. Thus, over our sample period governments responded to higher debt and to higher interest rates by reducing primary deficits. Moving across the table, we see this response is mainly the result of reductions in program spending. This suggests that increases in debt servicing costs have tended to "crowd out" program spending rather than "crowd in" revenues; indeed, the coefficient on INTEREST in the revenue column is the opposite of what we might expect, though it is very small.

The results presented in Table 5-1 are suggestive of a very strong influence of politics on fiscal policy in Canada. Based upon these results, we confidently reject any suggestion that "all political parties are alike", at least with respect to expenditure choices. Unfortunately for Canadian taxpayers, the argument that all parties are more alike with respect to the decision to raise taxes finds support in our estimates. Finally, on the basis of our results it is difficult to believe any claim from politicians that elections do not cause them to behave differently with respect to fiscal policy choices.

In Table 5-2 we look at the role of politics in a slightly different way. Here we make use of our definitions of fiscal stances discussed earlier. In particular, we define a "fiscal contraction" as being either a tight or a very

Table 5-2: Fiscal Expansions, Contractions, and Elections		
	Election Years	**Non-Election Years**
Frequency of Fiscal Expansions	38.9%	19.0%
Frequency of Fiscal Contractions	21.3%	34.4%

The frequency fiscal expansions in election years is calculated as (number of loose or very loose stances adopted in election years)/(number of election years). The frequency fiscal contractions in election years is calculated as (number of tight or very tight stances adopted in election years)/(number of election years). Neutral stances were observed 39.8% of the time in election years and 46.6% of the time in non-election years.

tight fiscal stance. Similarly, a "fiscal expansion" is defined as being either a loose or a very loose fiscal stance. With these definitions, we calculate the percentage of times that fiscal contractions and expansions have been adopted in election versus non-election years.

These data display a remarkable symmetry. Discretionary budget changes that have the effect of increasing the cyclically adjusted deficit (fiscal expansions) are more than twice as likely to occur in an election year than are discretionary changes that have the effect of reducing the deficit (fiscal contractions). In non-election years, discretionary policies aimed at reducing the size of the deficit are much more likely than policies aimed at increasing the deficit.

It is interesting that Alesina and Perotti do not find such a pattern in OECD countries. This pattern of increasing program spending (or, less often, cutting taxes) during election years and cutting program spending (or, more often, raising taxes) during non-election years may be a uniquely Canadian phenomenon. Another possibility, however, is that by failing to control for cross-country differences in monetary and exchange rate policies, and differences in electoral institutions, Alesina and Perotti fail to describe a more universal phenomenon.

PAST (IN)DISCRETIONS

CHAPTER SIX
WHAT HAVE WE LEARNED

In the previous chapters we undertook a fairly detailed analysis of the fiscal policy of both the federal and provincial governments over the period from 1962-1996. What have we learned from this exercise? The first part of this concluding chapter is devoted to addressing this question. More specifically, in the following section we provide a summary of what we think are some of the more important insights we have gained from our analysis. Having summarized our findings, we then turn our attention to possible directions for future research.

6.1 Summary of Findings
This section provides a brief summary of our major findings. It does so under six key areas.

6.1.1 Identifying Discretionary Policy
A theme underlying much of our analysis is that many factors affect the deficit and debt positions of governments but only some of these are in the control of governments: changes in spending and revenue due to discretionary policy choices. Many other factors affecting deficits and debt are not under the direct control of governments and are therefore not attributable to policy choices, at least contemporaneous ones. When characterizing and analyzing fiscal *policy*, it is clearly important to distinguish between these factors, and to recognize the interactions between them.

For example, in Chapter 2, we presented the "simple arithmetic" of the government budget constraint. That discussion revealed that one of the most important factors influencing the growth of government deficits and debt is the relative size of the interest rate paid on outstanding government debt and the rate of growth in the economy. For the most part, these crucial variables are beyond the control of governments in a small open economy such as Canada. Also from Chapter 2, we saw that since the early 1980s the interest rate on Canadian government debt has exceeded the rate of growth in the economy. Since that time, then, Canadian governments would have had to run primary surpluses – sometimes quite substantial primary surpluses – to prevent growth in their deficits and the rapid accumulation of debt. Primary surpluses require decisive discretionary fiscal policy actions to increase tax rates, and/or decrease expenditures. Were such actions taken? If so, when and how? To answer these questions, we needed to separate changes in revenues and expenditures arising from changes in economic conditions from those due to discretionary fiscal policy actions.

To do this, we relied on a relatively simple methodology – a methodology that has been used elsewhere to identify and evaluate the discretionary fiscal policy of OECD countries. Despite the methodology's simplicity, we showed that it did as good a job of identifying the discretionary fiscal policy choices of the federal government as more complicated and intensive approaches. This was important because the methodology we employed can just as easily be applied to data describing provincial government budgets as it can to data describing federal government budgets. More complicated and intensive approaches are far less amenable to application to provincial government budgets. The approach we used, then, allowed us to identify and evaluate the fiscal policies of all eleven fiscal authorities, the federal government and the governments of the ten provinces.

6.1.2 Bigger or Smaller Government?
Our central theme of distinguishing between those factors that are under the discretionary control of governments, and those that are not, played a key role in Chapter 4 where we sought to explicitly differentiate between discretionary and non-discretionary changes in fiscal stances. The goal here was not to identify fiscal changes that needed to be made to maintain a constant debt/GDP ratio – the issue of sustainability (which we summarize in section 6.1.4) – but rather to describe the nature of the fiscal choices that were actually made over the period 1962-96. In pursuit of this goal, we identified the *composition* of the discretionary fiscal stances adopted by the federal government and the ten provinces.

This exercise uncovered some fascinating regularities in fiscal policy. One of these regularities is that there has been a tendency on the part of Canadian governments, until very recently, to make discretionary fiscal choices that increased the size of government relative to the size of the economy. "Loose", or expansionary, fiscal policy which increases the size of the deficit can be accomplished in two ways – by increasing program expenditures or by cutting taxes. The former choice results in a larger government presence, the latter in a smaller presence. When Canadian governments have introduced expansionary fiscal policies, they have tended to do so by increasing program expenditures rather than by reducing tax rates. This is particularly the case for substantial, or what we called "very loose", episodes of fiscal expansion (where the discretionary increase in the deficit was over 1.5% of GDP). In these instances, discretionary increases in program expenditures typically made up more than 80% of the total increase in the deficit while tax reductions typically made up less than 20%. In fact, we could identify only nine cases of a Canadian government introducing a fiscal policy designed to substantially increase the size of its deficit mainly via tax cuts; this out of a sample of forty-two very loose fiscal stances and 385 stances overall. On the other hand, instances of discretionary policy intended to reduce the size of the deficit (contractionary, or "tight" fiscal policy) have typically been characterized by a much more balanced approach, with discretionary reductions in spending and increases in revenues of roughly equal magnitudes. Of the sixty-two instances of "very tight" fiscal policy we identified, twenty-four were dominated by expenditure cuts, twenty by tax increases, and eighteen by neither. Thus Canadian governments have tended to favour a balanced approach to fiscal policy changes only when the policy is to reduce the size of the deficit. A distinctly "unbalanced" approach in favour of increasing program spending has traditionally been favoured when the fiscal policy choice is to increase the size of the deficit.

This tendency to use expenditure-dominant fiscal policy to expand the size of the deficit and to use a more balanced fiscal policy to reduce it, leads inevitably to a growing share of GDP absorbed by government budgets. It suggests a very strong bias toward adopting fiscal policy that increases (or at least does not decrease) the role of the government in the economy. It also suggests that political considerations may play a key role in determining fiscal policy choices, a topic we discuss in more detail below.

6.1.3 More Recent Fiscal Choices, 1993-96

The tendency for Canadian fiscal policy to favour a balanced approach to deficit reduction changed abruptly in the early 1990s, when almost all Canadian governments embarked on very substantial fiscal retrenchments. For many governments, the tax gap between sustainable and actual tax rates turned negative for the first time in many years, and for the first time in many years the net debt/GDP ratio began to decline.[1] Over the period 1993-96 inclusive, the change in the primary deficit/GDP ratio due to discretionary policy choices ranged from a low of 1.83 percentage points of GDP in British Columbia to a high of 7.21 percentage points in

Saskatchewan. The federal government introduced policy changes that reduced its primary deficit/GDP ratio by 1.83 percentage points. Moreover, contrary to what has tended to happen in the past, these deficit reductions were largely led by cuts to program expenditures. Our results for Saskatchewan and Alberta were particularly interesting, as they seem to fly in the face of accepted wisdom. Popular perception seems to be that in the 1990s Saskatchewan relied heavily, compared in particular to Alberta, on revenue increases to deal with its fiscal problems. Our calculations show just the opposite.[2] By our calculations, the government of Saskatchewan led all Canadian governments in expenditure-led deficit reduction during the 1993-96 period. Alberta came in second.

The 1993-96 period was characterized by moderate, if not strong, economic growth and interest rates that were quite low by historical standards. The federal government's total deficit/GDP ratio declined by 2.63 percentage points over this period. Reductions in the provinces ranged from a low of 1.93 percentage points (British Columbia) to a high of 8.16 percentage points (Saskatchewan). While it is easy to observe the fall in total deficit/GDP ratios for the provinces and the federal government, as discussed above changes in the total deficit are due both to changes in economic conditions and due to discretionary policy changes. How much of the change in total deficit/GDP ratios was due to discretionary policy changes initiated over this period, and how much to fortuitous economic conditions?

Our calculations show that the large bulk of the decline in deficit/GDP ratios over this period was indeed due to discretionary government policy. For example, 70% of the reduction in the federal government's deficit that occurred from 1993-1996 arose from discretionary actions on the part of the federal government. As mentioned above, all of this, and more, was on the expenditure side of the budget. The remaining 30% of the deficit reduction was due to the effects of automatic stabilizers on revenues and expenditures, and the effect of falling interest rates on debt service costs. However, much of the federal government's discretionary expenditure reduction took the form of reduced transfers to the provinces – about one-third of the discretionary expenditure reductions on the part of the federal government were to provincial transfers.

The provinces turned out to be even more aggressive than the federal government in implementing discretionary decreases in their deficits. The proportion of the deficit reductions coming from discretionary actions on the part of provincial governments ranged from a low of 78% in Manitoba, to a high of 132% in Newfoundland! The estimate for Newfoundland is due to the fact that over the four year period 1993 to 1996, while the Newfoundland government introduced discretionary changes in fiscal policy designed to reduce the deficit/GDP ratio by about 3.5 percentage points, poor economic conditions in that province caused the deficit to fall by only 2.6 percentage points. Thus, the discretionary changes in fiscal policy instituted by the Newfoundland government were partly offset by the budgetary effects of poor economic conditions.

6.1.4 Sustainability and the "Fiscal Wall"

The crucial role played by interest and growth rates was also apparent in our discussion of the sustainability of fiscal policy in Chapter 3. There we saw that if the interest rate exceeds the growth rate in the economy, the tax/GDP ratio required to maintain program spending/GDP and prevent the debt/GDP ratio from growing – the so-called *sustainable tax rate* – grows larger, the larger is the existing level of debt. A positive gap between the sustainable tax rate and the actual tax rate in the economy (actual taxes collected/GDP), called the *tax gap*, is indicative of a fiscal position leading to an expanding debt/GDP ratio.

In Chapter 3 we saw that until very recently, for the past 25 years and for virtually every government in Canada, the tax gap has been consistently positive, as reflected in rising debt/GDP ratios. While the tax gap tended to grow and ebb with the business cycle – increasing with recessions and decreasing with recoveries – fiscal policy in Canada has been characterized by a stubbornly positive tax gap throughout the period we studied. Although the rate of growth in net debt/GDP tended to slow during economic upswings, it never turned negative, or even zero, until very recently, and then only for some governments. In the continued presence of a high interest rate on government debt relative to the rate of growth in the economy, the closing of the tax gap requires discretionary actions on the fiscal policy front to stem the rising debt tide, actions most governments in Canada seemed reluctant to take until the mid-1990s.

None of this, of course, is much of a surprise; the fact that net debt/GDP ratios have been growing over the past three decades is well known. What we did learn from our investigation is the magnitude of the changes in taxes and/or spending required to stop this growth, and something about the timing of the fiscal retrenchments undertaken by some of the governments. For the federal government, for example, the tax gap over the past two decades has averaged more than three percentage points. This means that an increase in federal taxes, or a decrease in federal expenditures, of more than three percentage points of GDP was required to stem the growth in the debt/GDP ratio. Since over this period federal taxes averaged 17% of GDP, halting the growth in debt required a substantial fiscal policy response; equivalent to an almost 20% increase in the tax burden.

The federal government finally took substantive action in this regard in 1996, the first time in over two decades that the tax gap turned negative and the net debt/GDP ratio began to fall from the lofty level of 73%. In 1996, the most recent year for which we are able to make the calculation, the federal tax gap was *minus* 1.4%. This means that in 1996 the federal government collected about $11 billion more in taxes than it needed to finance program spending and maintain the net debt/GDP ratio at its 1996 level. If maintained, this suggests a steady decline in the federal debt/GDP ratio.

As of 1996, when viewed in aggregate the provinces still had not turned the fiscal corner. The aggregate provincial tax gap remained positive, though lower than it had been in the past. This suggests continued, though slower, growth in the aggregate provincial net debt/GDP ratio over the short term. This is due in large part to the unsustainable fiscal policies being followed in the large provinces of British Columbia, Quebec and Ontario. In each of these provinces the actual tax rate in 1996 remained too low to finance program spending without increasing the debt/GDP ratio. Either tax increases or spending reductions are required for fiscal policy to become sustainable in those provinces. In British Columbia, the tax gap in 1996 was 3.5%, while in Ontario it was 0.5%, and in Quebec it was 0.8%. As of 1996, then, these provinces still had some way to go to stem the growth of debt relative to the size of the economy. For example, as of 1996, (assuming unchanged interest and growth rates) British Columbia would have had to increase taxes or decrease program spending by over $3.7 billion to stop the growth in its debt/GDP ratio; in Ontario the figure is $1.6 billion and in Quebec $1.4 billion.

Interestingly, we found that in the 1990s, smaller provinces were the first to move quickly and decisively to stem debt growth. Saskatchewan is particularly noteworthy here, having moved more quickly and decisively than any other province. This was due in large part to that nasty budget arithmetic. The smaller provinces had much higher debt/GDP ratios entering the 1990s and, with interest rates in excess of GDP growth rates, this meant they have very sustainable tax rates. These provinces really had no choice but to act decisively on the fiscal front, and act they did.

Figure 6-1 offers a bit of evidence on the question of whether there exists a "fiscal wall" – that is, a level of net debt relative to GDP beyond which a government might be forced to act strongly and decisively to prevent further debt accumulation. The figure compares the sum of the fiscal impulses imposed by each government over the 1993-96 period – data taken from the first column of Table 4-10 – to the size of each government's debt/GDP ratio in 1993. The idea is to ask to what extent the level of debt in 1993 can account for the strength of the fiscal retrenchment undertaken by that government over the next four years.

Figure 6-1 Hitting the Fiscal Wall?

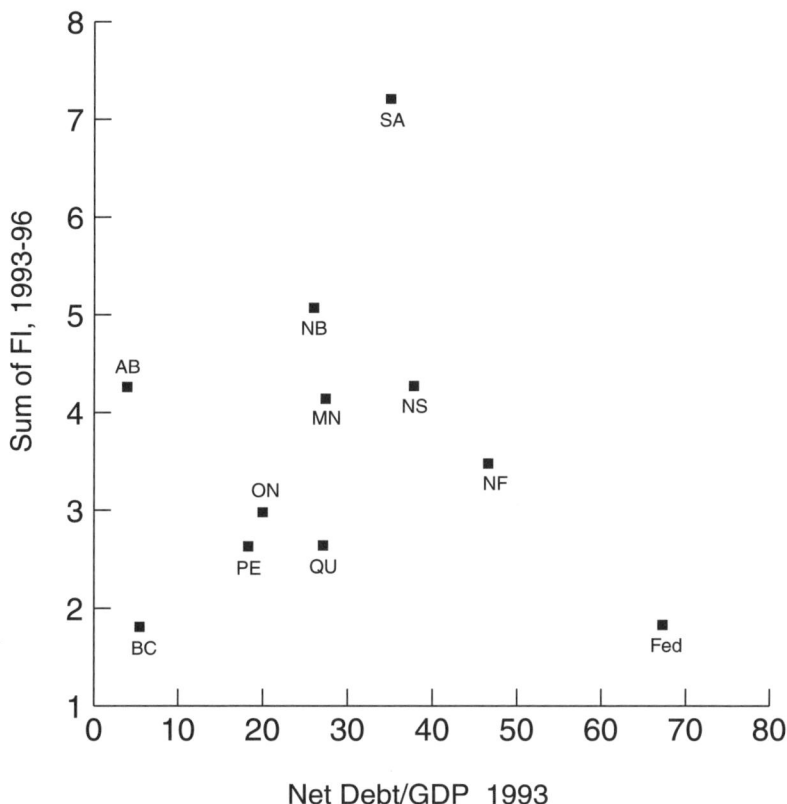

Certainly, factors other than the level of debt in 1993 likely played a significant role in determining the fiscal policy each province chose to impose over the next four years. Moreover, we are not suggesting that the level of debt defining the "fiscal wall" is common to all governments. It is unlikely, for example, that a large, industrially diversified province like Ontario would hit a fiscal wall at the same level of debt as a province like Newfoundland. The figure is suggestive, however, of a positive relationship between the level of debt and the discretionary fiscal policy response of provincial governments to that debt. Ignoring for the moment the federal government and Alberta, there is a pronounced positive relationship between the size of the fiscal impulses over the 1993-1996 period and the net debt/GDP ratio - the larger is a government's debt, the closer it is to its own fiscal wall and the stronger is the fiscal policy response.

One obvious outlier from this relationship is the federal government. In 1993 the federal government had the highest debt of all eleven governments and yet introduced the smallest discretionary policy actions. One of the reasons that the federal debt/GDP ratio can be so much higher than provincial debt/GDP ratios, aside from its more diversified tax base, is that the federal government has a financing option available to it that provinces do not have, namely monetization. The federal government can simply print more money and inflate the debt away in real terms. The availability of this financing option frees the federal government from the discipline imposed by credit rating agencies downgrading domestic currency debt.[3] It is not surprising, then, that the federal government might be an outlier in this relationship.

The fact that Alberta introduced a much more stringent fiscal retrenchment than might be expected given its low debt/GDP ratio, suggests that the rate of change in a province's debt/GDP ratio, aside from just the level of that ratio, may play a role in determining the size of the fiscal response. Between 1989 and 1993, Alberta went from a net asset position equal to 10.9% of GDP to a net debt of 3.9% of GDP, a turnaround of 14.8 percentage points of GDP in just four years. Perhaps, then, the amount of debt *recently* accumulated played a role in determining Alberta's fiscal policies over the 1993-96 period. To investigate this question, and to see if it was true for all governments, we ran a regression explaining the sum of the fiscal impulses imposed by each government over the 1993-96 period (FISUM) as a function of the change in each province's net debt/GDP ratio over the 1989-93 period (DEBTC) and the level of debt in 1993 (DEBT). In recognition of the fact the federal government's behaviour seems to be different from provincial behaviour, we also included a dummy variable for the federal government (FED). The results are (standard errors are in parentheses);

$$FISUM = 1.73 + 0.03*DEBT + 0.15*DEBTC - 4.06*FED$$
$$(1.00) \quad (0.03) \quad (0.08) \quad (1.87)$$
$$\overline{R}^2 = 0.36$$

While we stress that other factors most certainly played a role in determining fiscal policy choices over this period, and that we are well aware that we have very few observations, the results of this simple cross-sectional regression are suggestive nonetheless. The coefficient on the DEBTC variable indicates that recent growth in the debt/GDP ratio has indeed caused governments to impose larger fiscal retrenchments than they would otherwise. In fact, this seems to have played a larger role than the level of debt. The coefficient on the dummy variable for the federal government indicates that it imposed a much less stringent retrenchment than it would have had to impose if it was a province with the same debt/GDP ratio. If the federal government was subject to the same borrowing constraints as provinces, these results suggest that it would have cut its deficit/GDP ratio by an additional four percentage points of GDP over the 1993-96 period.

6.1.5 Are There Preferred Approaches to Deficit Reduction?

A question that often arises in this era of fiscal restraint is whether a particular approach to deficit reduction is likely to be more or less "successful" than another approach. As we discussed in Chapter 4, the answer to this question depends critically upon how one defines "successful." One approach is to look at the "staying power" of fiscal retrenchments. Using this standard, a fiscal retrenchment is successful if it results in low deficits for a number of years following the retrenchment. Are expenditure-dominant fiscal retrenchments (where expenditure cuts are the dominant source of the reduction in the deficit) more or less successful, by this standard, than revenue-dominant fiscal retrenchments? Given the recent change in the approach Canadian governments have taken to fiscal retrenchments, this is an extremely important question.

We investigated this question in two ways. The first involved looking at the characteristics of what we called 'very tight' fiscal episodes for the federal government and all of the provinces. If a very tight fiscal episode is followed in the next three years by primary deficits that were below the initial deficit by 1.5% of GDP (on average) we deemed this to be a successful fiscal retrenchment – one with staying power – otherwise, it was labeled as unsuccessful. This approach was suggested, and applied to OECD data, by Alesina and Perrotti.[4] They concluded that expenditure-dominant fiscal retrenchments tended to be more successful. We undertook a similar analysis of federal and provincial fiscal retrenchments in Canada. Our results confirmed what Alesina and Perrotti found for OECD countries: successful retrenchments tended to be dominated by expenditure cuts, while unsuccessful retrenchments tended to be dominated by revenue increases. This suggest that the expenditure dominated fiscal retrenchments of the 1990s have a good chance of "sticking."

However, as we discussed in Chapter 4, we do not have complete faith in this approach to identifying successful retrenchments, at least for Canada. We therefore approached the issue in a different way; a way that we think gets more to the crux of the matter. Using a simple but standard approach, we investigated the *direction of causality* between government expenditures and revenues. More specifically, we investigated whether taxes "cause" spending, or whether spending "causes" taxes. The former, called "tax and spend" behavior, means that when governments raise revenues to reduce the primary deficit, expenditures in subsequent periods tend to rise, reversing the original fiscal retrenchment. "Tax and spend" behavior by governments is thus unlikely to lead to a long lasting reduction in the deficit/GDP ratio.

We found strong evidence that the federal government has indeed tended to engage in "tax and spend" behavior but has not exhibited "spend and tax" behaviour. This suggests that for the federal government, revenue dominant fiscal retrenchments – deficit reduction via tax increases – are not likely to be long lasting since such tax increases have typically been followed by spending increases. Thus, the reduction in the deficit is only temporary. Cutting federal program spending, on the other hand, will prove more likely to be associated with a lasting reduction in the federal deficit. We therefore find support some for the federal government's recent policy of relying heavily on expenditure cuts to reduce its deficit. With respect to the provinces, however, we found no evidence suggestive of causation in either direction. Alternative methods of deficit reduction all seem equally capable (or incapable) of resulting in a lasting reduction in provincial deficits.

6.1.6 Political Influences

Our finding that Canadian governments tended to opt for fiscal policy choices that increased government's share of the economy suggests, as we noted above, political influences on fiscal policy choices. In our more detailed examination of the fiscal policy choices made by the federal government and the governments of Ontario and Alberta, we found numerous instances when it seemed that political considerations had played a key role. However, it is one thing to provide anecdotal evidence in this regard, and quite another to uncover systematic regularities. We turned to this issue in Chapter 5.

Our investigation focused on two broad elements in the political economy of fiscal policy. The first arises from the obvious desire on the part of politicians to get re-elected. This has several implications for fiscal policy; the one we focused on is the extent to which impending elections affect fiscal policy choices. As such, we looked for so-called *opportunistic* responses on the part of policy-makers to the timing of elections. The second avenue we investigated concerns the extent to which the ideological affiliation of the governing party affects fiscal policy choices. Here we looked for *partisan* effects, or differences in the fiscal policy choices of political parties.

When attempting to identify both opportunistic and partisan influences on fiscal policy, we were once again cognizant of the need to distinguish between discretionary and non-discretionary changes. Politically motivated fiscal policy, for either opportunistic or partisan reasons, obviously involves discretionary decisions. Our efforts to identify the discretionary policy changes introduced by the federal and provincial governments served us well here.

What did we find? First, our analysis indicated the presence of a very pronounced electoral, or opportunistic, cycle in the fiscal policy of Canadian governments. In election years, Canadian governments have shown a very strong tendency to initiate expansionary, or loose, fiscal policy via discretionary increases in the primary deficit/GDP ratio. Indeed, on average governments have adopted expansionary (loose) discretionary fiscal policy in election years and contractionary (tight) discretionary fiscal policy in non-election years. Across all eleven governments, discretionary fiscal expansions were more than twice as likely to occur in election years than non-election years, while discretionary fiscal contractions were more than one and one-half times more likely to occur during non-election years than election years. Moreover, we found that elections are associated with both increased program spending and more moderate tax increases, with a marked tendency to rely more heavily on expenditure increases. This provides some evidence that Canadian governments have sought to "buy" votes via expenditure increases in election years.

We also found strong evidence of partisan effects on the fiscal policy choices of Canadian governments. In particular, governments we have identified with a "left wing" fiscal ideology tended to engage in looser fiscal policy than so-called "right wing" governments. Indeed, while the latter have tended to initiate fiscal policies that on average were associated with a discretionary decrease in the primary deficit/GDP ratio, the former have initiated fiscal policies that on average were associated with no change in the primary deficit/GDP ratio.

An interesting by-product of our empirical investigation of political influences on fiscal policy is that, after controlling for partisan and opportunistic effects, we found debt service costs have tended to decrease, or "crowd out" government expenditures. Thus, faced with rising debt servicing costs, Canadian governments have typically responded by cutting program expenditures rather than increasing taxes.

The conclusion that politics is alive and well in Canada, and has had a significant and pronounced impact on fiscal policy, may come as no surprise to most Canadians. However, we are not aware of any previous systematic empirical investigation of the phenomenon, and even we were surprised by the extent and magnitude of the opportunistic and partisan influences. A famous quote by the political economist Anthony Downs suggests that "parties formulate policies in order to win elections, rather than win elections in order to formulate policies."[5] Our finding that both opportunistic and partisan considerations have a major impact on fiscal policy suggests that in Canada, political parties have tended to do both.

6.2 Final Thoughts

The purpose of this volume was to analyze the fiscal policy choices of Canadian governments since the 1960s, both federal and provincial, over time and across jurisdictions. We feel as though we have just scratched the surface of this important subject. Nonetheless, we feel we have come a fair distance and have gained some important insights into fiscal policy making in Canada.

We have stressed throughout the monograph that comparing raw budget data can give misleading and inappropriate results, but that some fairly straightforward adjustments can be used to clarify the nature of fiscal policy. It is particularly important in this regard to distinguish between discretionary and non-discretionary, or cyclical, changes in fiscal policy.

Much work needs to be done. We still do not have a strong understanding of the characteristics of "optimal" fiscal policy, with particular regard to things like the debt/GDP ratio. Also, we do not have a full understanding of the politics of fiscal policy-making. In particular, to the economist it is rather puzzling that some Canadian governments, most particularly the federal government but some of the provinces as well, ignored the "simple arithmetic" of government finances for so long. Why did these governments wait until debt levels reached arguably "crisis" levels before acting?[6] We also did not explore the very important questions of the interaction between monetary and fiscal policy nor the role that budget making institutions, norms, and conventions can play in the determination and implementation of fiscal policy.[7]

While more work needs to be done, it is our hope that the perspective taken in this monograph has uncovered some new and interesting insights that will change the way that we view fiscal policy in Canada, both historically and in the future.

ENDNOTES

Chapter 1

1. Very recently, a number of provinces have introduced legislation of this sort. New Brunswick introduced legislation in 1993 that restricted the size of its deficit. Alberta, Saskatchewan, and Manitoba all followed in 1995 with legislation designed to influence budgeting behaviour and restrict the use of deficit finance.
2. See, for example, Persson and Svensson (1989).
3. See Tabellini and Alesina (1990).
4. Our approach is due to Blanchard (1993).
5. See, again, Blanchard (1993).

Chapter 2

1. Allowing government to run periodic budget deficits and surpluses is beneficial for at least three reasons. First, the power to deficit finance enables governments to allow automatic stabilizers to work freely. Thus during an economic recession, when tax revenues fall, an alternative to raising tax rates or cutting program expenditures in order to balance the budget is to deficit finance expenditures. It is important to note, however, that the effective operation of automatic stabilizers does not prohibit budget surpluses nor does it require budget deficits. It only requires that budget deficits (surpluses) grow larger (smaller) during recessions and grow smaller (larger) during expansions. Thus, over the course of the business cycle, there is no reason to suggest that deficits should exceed surpluses leading to a permanent level of accumulated debt. Similarly, the "tax smoothing" argument for maintaining a constant tax rate in the face of a variable tax base does not suggest that cyclically-induced deficits should exceed surpluses. It is not, then, an argument for maintaining a permanent amount of debt. Finally, the power to run budget imbalances enables governments to

apply aggregate demand stabilization policies. Thus the government in an economy experiencing inflationary pressures might choose to run a budget surplus while the government of an economy in recession might choose to run a deficit. If government chooses to use stabilization policies to smooth both booms and recessions, the use of counter-cyclical stabilization policies do not imply the existence of a permanent level of debt.

2. In a small open economy, firms can borrow abroad as well as domestically. As a result, the domestic interest rate is largely determined by exogenous factors and domestic investment may be less affected by domestic government debt than we have suggested. However, the evidence provided by Feldstein and Horioka (1980) suggests a close connection between domestic investment and private domestic saving despite capital mobility. A possible explanation for this is that domestic firms have limited access to capital markets (something that is certainly true of small firms) and thus must rely on retained earnings. Since retained earnings are included in measures of domestic saving, we get a positive relation between investment and saving even in a small open economy. Thus if government competes with such firms for domestic savings, lower economic growth results. A second channel through which increased government debt leads to slower economic growth in a small open economy is via a risk premium added to the domestic interest rate. Such a risk premium arises due to international lenders' concerns about the exchange rate effects of higher government debt.

3. Assume factors of production earn their marginal product. The marginal product of capital (MP_K) can be expressed as capital's share of total income ($MP_K \bullet K/Y$) divided by the capital-output ratio (K/Y). In Canada, the gross return to capital is about one-quarter of output and the capital-output ratio is in the vicinity of two. This makes the implied gross marginal product of capital equal to about 12.5 percent. If we assume depreciation of capital of about 10 percent, net marginal product of capital is about 2.5 percent. Thus each dollar of capital raises gross domestic product by 12.5 cents and net domestic product by 2.5 cents. In Canada, the debts of the federal and provincial governments combined is about 100% of GDP. If we assume government debt replaces private investment dollar-for-dollar, eliminating this net debt would increase GDP by 12.5% and net national product by 2.5%.

4. See Dahlby (1994).

5. See Elmendorf and Mankiw (1998) for similar calculations relevant to the United States. They conclude that U.S. government debt, which, as a fraction of GDP, is only half the size of Canadian government

debt, imposes a cost of about $300 billion per year or $1000 per person per year.

6. For different perspectives on what the economically optimal level of government debt might be see Aiyagari and McGrattan (1995) and Scarth and Jackson (1998).

7. See Hettich and Winer (1988) and Gillespie (1991).

8. As we explained in section 2.3, it is generally believed that high levels of government debt cause interest rates to be higher, and economic growth rates to be lower, than otherwise. In 1980, however, government debts in Canada were not at high levels so it is unlikely that fiscal policy choices of that period can be faulted for the reversal in the relative magnitudes of these variables.

9. This was true as well prior to the 1960s during non-war and non-depression years. See Gillespie (1991) for data on federal government revenues, expenditures, deficits, and debt from 1868 to 1989.

Chapter 3

1. Blanchard (1993).

2. An appendix at the end of the chapter provides a formal derivation of this condition.

3. Curtis (1997) also calculates tax gaps using the Blanchard method but does so for the federal government only.

Chapter 4

1. See Blanchard (1993).

2. See Blanchard (1993). Alesina and Perotti (1995, 1997) and McDermott and Wescott (1996) recently used a similar approach to analyse the fiscal policy of OECD countries.

3. The adjustment is not exact because government spending is thought to grow at a different rate of inflation than GDP. Another relevant factor is the lack of full inflation indexing in the income tax system. Using ratios to GDP also ignores the influence demographic changes might have on the deficit. For example, an aging population puts greater strains on government expenditures – especially on health care and pension expenditures – and slows economic growth. However, demographic effects on the budget move slowly enough that they wouldn't have a substantial impact on an indicator of changes in discretionary fiscal policy from one year to the next, the creation of which is our goal.

4. To the extent that fiscal choices affect interest rates by causing risk premiums on government debt to change, this assumption will understate the influence of fiscal policy on budget changes. It is like-

ly the case, however, that changes in risk premiums move slowly enough that they would not have a substantial impact on an indicator of changes in discretionary fiscal policy from one year to the next.

5. Research at the Bank of Canada on the appropriate method for calculating estimates of potential output at the national level is extensive and on-going. For a review, see St-Amant and van Norden (1997). Recent research has been in the direction of multivariate filters. While fewer data series are required in this approach relative to the older production function approach, it nonetheless relies on long, and preferably high frequency, time series. Relevant time series on a provincial basis are available for much shorter periods and only on an annual basis. None of the published research at the Bank of Canada has been directed toward the question of the appropriate way of modifying these approaches to estimating potential output at sub-national levels.

6. These data are from Tables 9.1 and 9.3, *The National Finances*, Canadian Tax Foundation, 1994.

7. For a thorough description and discussion of the system of intergovernmental transfers in Canada, see Boadway and Hobson (1993).

8. We experimented with several alternative assumptions regarding how to allocate federal-provincial transfers with no substantial changes in the results.

9. See Alesina and Perotti (1995).

10. Alesina and Perotti (1995) find that their results, for OECD countries, are also not sensitive to switching to this definition.

11. See Kneebone (1994)

12. See Alesina and Perotti (1995, 1997). From our Table 4-2 we see that the average very tight stance in Canada over our sample period was 2.5% of GDP (versus 2.6% of GDP in Alesina and Perotti's sample of OECD countries). Thus the criteria for success employed by Alesina and Perotti allows for some "slippage" in the deficit reduction effort in the sense that an average sized very tight stance need only cause the deficit to remain lower by 1.5% of GDP. To reduce the amount of "slippage" allowed, we tried using 2.0 rather than 1.5 in the definition of success. This choice, indeed even increasing it to 2.5, while obviously decreasing the number of "successful", and increasing the number of "unsuccessful" retrenchments, has no qualitative effect on our conclusion. Alesina and Perotti also employ a measure of success involving the amount by which a jurisdiction's debt/GDP falls over the 3 years following a very tight stance. They note that their conclusions are not effected by this alternative criteria for defining success. We use the deficit/GDP criteria since data on debt/GDP ratios for provinces is available only from 1970.

13. See Government of Ontario (1996).

14. Although the government of Saskatchewan introduced policies that had the effect of reducing its tax revenue to GDP ratio over the 1993-96 period, it had earlier, in 1992, introduced a number of increases in tax rates that substantially increased its ratio of tax revenue to GDP. These included a 10% surtax on personal income, an increase in the corporate tax rate, an increase in the provincial sales tax rate from 7% to 9%, a broadened sales tax base, and increased tax rates on gasoline and tobacco.

15. The well-known cuts to the personal income tax rate in Ontario did not begin until the 1996 tax year when the personal income tax rate was cut from 58% to 56% of the federal rate. The larger cuts that are scheduled to reduce it to 38.5% of the federal rate in 1999 do not show up in our data. Prior to these cuts, Ontario's personal income tax rate had been increased from 53% to 58% of the federal rate and a substantial surtax was introduced in 1993.

16. The remainder of this section relates our measures of fiscal impulses to policy choices made by budget-makers. Excellent sources describing these choices are Perry (1989) and McMillan (1991). The rest of this section relies heavily on these sources.

17. Consider one anecdotal illustration of this chilling effect: In 1993 Finance Minister Paul Martin paid a private visit to Solange Denis, who delivered the famous "Goodbye Charlie Brown" speech to Prime Minister Mulroney, to gain her approval for the budget measures he planned to introduce in the forthcoming budget.

18. In 1990, Ontario's unemployment rate had increased by 1.2 percentage points from the previous year. This compares to an increase of just 0.1 percentage points in the rest of the country. The following year, Ontario's unemployment rate increased a further 3.3 percentage points versus 1.5 percentage points in the rest of the country.

19. The 1975 provincial sales tax cut was coordinated by the federal government in an attempt to stimulate the economy. All provinces but Alberta (which had, and has, no provincial sales tax) participated in the plan. As a result, a positive discretionary fiscal impulse is typically found in the provincial budget data.

20. Kneebone and McKenzie (1998) report that over the period 1961-95, Alberta's real GDP was negatively correlated with real GDP in Ontario and four other provinces.

21. These prices were the Edmonton price for crude oil and equivalents.

22. For a chronology of events during the period leading up to and following the NEP see Doern and Toner (1985).

23. As well as Perry (1989) and McMillan (1991), which we cited earlier

as valuable sources for descriptions of discretionary fiscal choices, see Boothe (1995) and Mansell (1997) for a descriptions of these choices in Alberta.
24. Doern and Toner (1985).
25. Boothe (1995).

Chapter 5
1. Seminal papers in this area include Nordhaus (1975), Lindbeck (1976), and Hibbs (1977, 1987). For a recent survey of this literature, see Alesina, Roubini, and Cohen (1997).
2. For an example of this approach applied to Canadian provincial data, see Reid (1998).
3. The effect fiscal policy has on the economy depends in large part on monetary policy choices. In small open economies, the choice of exchange rate regime and the degree of central bank intervention in foreign exchange markets plays a key role in determining the effect fiscal policy has on the economy and on the question of what policy instruments authorities use to influence economic outcomes. Finally, the characteristics of electoral systems have been identified by many in this literature as playing an important role in determining fiscal policy choices (see, for example, Persson and Svensson (1989)).
4. We also created a dummy variable defining minority governments. However, our sample contains only 19 observations of minority governments. We considered this too small a number to draw inferences.

Chapter 6
1. As discussed in section 6.1.4 and Chapter 3, the sustainable tax rate is the revenue/GDP ratio required to maintain current program spending while maintaining the current net debt/GDP ratio. The actual tax rate is simply actual tax revenues as a percentage of GDP.
2. Boothe and Reid (1998) provides some support for our view that Saskatchewan was much more active on the expenditure front than commonly perceived.
3. For a discussion, see Kneebone (1994).
4. See Alesina and Perrotti (1995, 1997).
5. Downs (1957, page 28).
6. On this issue, see Alesina and Drazen (1991) and Drazen and Grilli (1993).
7. On the latter issue, see Hettich and Winer (1995), von Hagen and Harden (1995), and Bruce, Kneebone, and McKenzie (1997).

REFERENCES

Aiyagari, R. and E. McGrattan (1995) "The Optimum Quantity of Debt," Federal Reserve Bank of Minneapolis Research Department Staff Report 203.

Alesina, A. and A. Drazen (1991) "Why are Stabilizations Delayed?," *American Economic Review*, 81: 1170-1188.

Alesina, A. and R. Perotti (1995) "Fiscal Expansions and Adjustments in OECD Countries," *Economic Policy*, 20, 207-248.

Alesina, A. and R. Perotti (1997) "Fiscal Adjustments in OECD Countries: Composition and Macroeconomic Effects," IMF Staff Papers, 44(2), 210-248.

Alesina, A., N. Roubini, and G. Cohen (1997) *Political Cycles and the Macroeconomy*, MIT Press, Cambridge, MA.

Blanchard, O. (1993) "Suggestions for a New Set of Fiscal Indicators," in *The Political Economy of Government Debt*, H.A.A. Verbon and F.A.A.M van Winden (editors), North-Holland.

Boadway, R. and P. Hobson (1993) "Intergovernmental Fiscal Relations in Canada," Canadian Tax Paper No. 94, Canadian Tax Foundation.

Boothe, P. (1995) *The Growth of Government Spending in Alberta*, Canadian Tax Paper No. 100, Canadian Tax Foundation.

Boothe, P. and B. Reid (1998) "Comparing Deficit Reduction in BC, Alberta and Saskatchewan", presented at The Great Experiment:

Deficit Reduction in Western Canada, a conference sponsored by the Institute of Public Economics, Edmonton.

Bruce, C.J., R.D. Kneebone and K.J. McKenzie (1997) *A Government Reinvented: A Study of Alberta's Deficit Elimination Program*, Oxford University Press, Toronto.

Curtis, D. (1997) "The Struggle to Control Federal Deficits and the Debt in Canada, 1980-97", *Canadian Business Economics*, 6(1): 20-31.

Dahlby, B. (1994) "The Distortionary Effect of Rising Taxes," in *Deficit Reduction: What Pain? What Gain?*, W. Robson and W. Scarth (eds), C.D. Howe Institute Policy Study 23, 43-72.

Dixit, A. (1996) *The Making of Economic Policy: A Transaction-Cost Politics Perspective*, The MIT Press, Cambridge MA.

Doern, G.B. and G. Toner (1985) *The Politics of Energy*, Methuen, Toronto.

Downs, A. (1957) *An Economic Theory of Democracy*, Harper & Row, New York.

Drazen, A. and V. Grilli (1993) "The Benefit of Crises for Economic Reforms," *American Economic Review*, 83 (3): 598-607.

Elmendorf, D.W. and N.G. Mankiw (1998) "Government Debt," National Bureau of Economic Research Working Paper 6470.

Feldstein, M. and C. Horioka (1980) "Domestic Saving and International Capital Flows," *Economic Journal* 90, 314-329.

Gillespie, W.I. (1991) *Tax, Borrow and Spend: Financing Federal Spending in Canada, 1867-1990*, Carleton University Press, Ottawa.

Government of Ontario (1996) *Economic Policies for Jobs and Growth*, 1996 Ontario Budget, Queen's Park, Toronto.

Hettich, W. and S. Winer (1988) "Economic and Political Foundations of Tax Structure," *American Economic Review*, 78: 701-712.

Hettich, W. and S. Winer (1995) "Decision Externalities, Economic Efficiency and Institutional Responses", *Canadian Public Policy*, 21(3): 344-361.

Hibbs, D. (1977), "Political Parties and Macroeconomic Policy," *American Political Science Review 71*, 1467-87.

Hibbs, D. (1987), *The American Political Economy: Electoral Policy and Macroeconomics in Contemporary America*, Harvard University Press, Cambridge MA.

Kneebone, R. (1994) "Deficits and Debt in Canada: Some Lessons from Recent History," *Canadian Public Policy*, 20(2), 152-164.

Kneebone, R. and K. McKenzie (1998) "Stabilizing Features of Fiscal Policy in Canada," in *Fiscal Targets and Economic Growth*, T. Courchene and T. Wilson (eds), John Deutsch Institute for the Study of Economic Policy, Kingston, Ontario, 191-235.

Lindbeck, A. (1976), "Stabilization Policies in Open Economies with Endogenous Politicians," *American Economic Review Papers and Proceedings*, 1-19.

Mansell, R. (1997) "Fiscal Restructuring in Alberta: An Overview of the Program and the Economic and Political Environment," in C. Bruce, R. Kneebone, and K. McKenzie (eds), *A Government Reinvented: A Study of Alberta's Deficit Elimination Program*, Oxford University Press.

McDermott, C.J. and R.F. Westcott (1996) "An Empirical Analysis of Fiscal Adjustments," IMF Working Paper WP/96/59.

McMillan, M.L. (1991) *Provincial Public Finances: Plaudits, Problems and Prospects*, Canadian Tax Paper No. 91, Toronto.

Nordhaus, W. (1975) "The Political Business Cycle," *Review of Economic Studies*, 42, 169-190.

Perry, J.H. (1989) *A Fiscal History of Canada – The Postwar Years*, Canadian Tax Paper No. 85, Canadian Tax Foundation.

Persson, T. and L. Svennson (1989) "Why a Stubborn Conservative Would Run a Deficit: Policy with Time Inconsistent Preferences," *Quarterly Journal of Economics*.

Reid, B. (1998) "Endogenous Elections, Electoral Budget Cycles and Canadian Provincial Governments", *Public Choice* 97: 35-48.

Sargent, T. (1986) "Interpreting the Reagan Deficits", *Federal Reserve Bank of San Francisco Quarterly Review*, Fall.

Scarth, W. and H. Jackson (1998) "The Target Debt-to-GDP Ratio: How Big Should It Be? and How Quickly Should We Approach It?" in *Fiscal Targets and Economic Growth*, T. Courchene and T. Wilson (eds), John Deutsch Institute for the Study of Economic Policy, Kingston, Ontario, 271-295.

St-Amant, P. and S. van Norden (1997) "Measurement of the Output Gap: A Discussion of Recent Research at the Bank of Canada", *Bank of Canada Technical Report No. 79*, August.

Tabellini, G. and A. Alesina (1990) "Voting on the Budget Deficit," *American Economic Review*, Volume 80 (1): 37-49.

von Hagen J. and I. Harden (1995), "Budget Processes and Commitment to Fiscal Discipline," *European Economic Review* (39), 771-779.